# JOHN HUNT MORGAN AND HIS GREAT RAID

## WILLIAM WOODROW SLIDER

Editors:
John Wesley Slider
Robert MacGregor Slider

Contributions by:
John Wesley Slider

Copyright © 2012 John Wesley Slider

All rights reserved.

ISBN: 1470105292
ISBN-13: 978-1470105297

## AUTHOR'S DEDICATION

To my father and mother, John Wiley Slider and Mamie Osman Slider, in sincere appreciation.

# CONTENTS

|  |  |  |
|---|---|---|
|  | Editors' Forward | i |
|  | Introduction | lii |
| 1 | The Thunderbolt of the Confederacy | 1 |
| 2 | Shiloh | 11 |
| 3 | Stones River | 21 |
| 4 | The Christmas Raid | 41 |
| 5 | Reasons for the Great Raid | 55 |
| 6 | Through Kentucky | 65 |
| 7 | Crossing at Brandenburg | 79 |
| 8 | Through Indiana | 85 |
| 9 | The End in Ohio | 99 |
| 10 | Results of the Raid | 115 |
| 11 | The End of the Trail | 119 |
|  | Original Bibliography | 129 |
|  | About the Author and Editors | 131 |

## EDITORS' FORWARD

This book is based on our father's dissertation for his Master of Arts in History from the University of Louisville in 1946. At the time he was serving as the pastor of Brandenburg Methodist Church — the little town that is mentioned in the history quite often.

Most people know our father as a gifted pastor and preacher. This dissertation reveals much of our father's other passions. He enjoyed history and the military.

We have added some material and some updated research to this book, but we believe that our additions add to rather than detract from our father's original work. We hope you enjoy our efforts.

John Wesley Slider
Robert MacGregor Slider
Louisville, Kentucky
February 2012

## INTRODUCTION

The Army of the United States has recently announced the incorporation of all cavalry units into the Armored Forces. The Horse Cavalry as a separate arm will cease to exist except for one regiment to be kept for show purposes. It is with a touch of nostalgia that we see the end of an arm of the services that has been tried over and over again in the heat of battle and has distinguished itself forever in the halls of history. Custer, Stuart, Sheridan, and Green have ridden into Valhalla never to be reincarnated.

It is in part with a wistful glance at the past and a desire to pay honor to a gallant service that I write upon the subject of one of the most outstanding cavalry leaders produced, not only in this country, but in the history of warfare. Sentiment alone is not reason for this study, but the desire for an understanding of military history and the development of tactics are other important reasons.

It is unquestionable fact that cavalry played an important part in the American Civil War. These cavalry men were not only to serve as scouts, but to act as infantry, to cover military movements, to destroy the lines of communication, to burn stores, to tear up lines of railway, to gather supplies, to fight gunboats, and capture transports; all these without equipment of any kind except their horses, their arms and some horse artillery of limited range (Young, p4).

The story of John Morgan holds a certain fascination because of his introduction of lightning war. It was he who originated the penetrating sweep into enemy territory, hold if possible, fall back if necessary. He drove a spearhead into the opposing country and then, from that central thrust, sent out many smaller detachments in order to completely disrupt the enemy's communications and strategy.

In John Hunt Morgan we also find several other points of interest. Under his command were many of the men of Kentucky who went to war for the South. He made two raids of over a thousand miles into enemy territory and carried the war farther into the North than any other general. There is a monument at New Lisbon, Ohio, that marks Morgan's northernmost strike.

This period of the Confederate cavalry is of interest, too, because of the underlying military plan that sent Morgan on his famous raid. Much is written of the activities of Northern troops in the Confederacy, and her we find an instance of comparison on Morgan's regiments as they rode through the North.

In this study of Morgan we also find marvelous records of endurance and marching. It is possible that he made the longest sustained march in the history of the world. True, Genghis Khan's Orkhons, Subotai, and Chepe Noyon, covered 4,000 miles with 20,000 men, but not in a sustained march.

The reception of the raiders in Indiana and Ohio also sheds light on the state of feeling in the North. Many Northerners were persuaded that the Copperhead and Anti-War element in the North were tremendous and far-reaching. The grim reception given Morgan is one of the only genuine indicators of the real feeling in the North. For example, at Cincinnati three times during the night General Morgan changed guides, and each time it was necessary by open or covert threat to force an enemy to lead the column (Young p385).

Finally, Morgan's raid is and will probably forever remain a part of the folklore of the War of the Rebellion. It is told and retold in a hundred different ways. Confusion and error creep into the stories that malign either one side or the other. What is the real story? The following pages will try to tell it.

# 1 THE THUNDERBOLT OF THE CONFEDERACY

There was in John Hunt Morgan and his deeds something appealing to the people. He was killed on a rain-swept morning during the closing months of the war. After his death the pride and the spirit of the South was never quite the same again (Holland, p17). It is true that the tide of John Morgan's success seemed to parallel that of the cause that he represented.

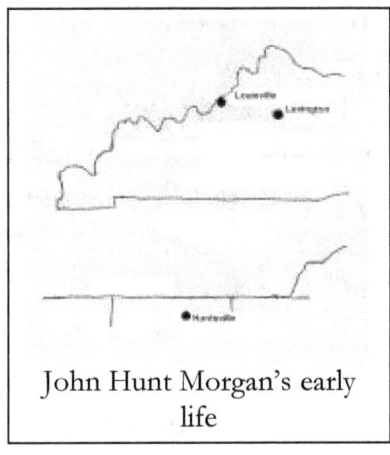

John Hunt Morgan's early life

John Hunt Morgan was born in Alabama at Huntsville, June 1, 1825. He was one of ten children born to Calvin and Henrietta Hunt Morgan. His mother's father was John Wesley

Hunt, one of the early founders of Lexington, Kentucky and one of the first millionaires in what was then considered the West.

John's paternal grandfather had settled his family in Huntsville and established a cotton business. A downturn in that industry placed the family in financial difficulties. His father, Luther Morgan, a pharmacist, lost the family's home in 1831, when his business failed.

John Morgan was four-years-old when the family moved to Lexington, Kentucky, and here his early training was received. At seventeen he was admitted to Transylvania College, but was he was suspended at the end of his second year for dueling with a fraternity brother.

After leaving Transylvania, he spent his time in the general pastimes of ante-bellum Kentucky - dancing, dueling, and drinking. There were many social activities to interest the blue-bloods of the area and they had little trouble finding the means for occupying their time.

Then came 1846 and the war with Mexico. John Morgan was twenty-one and eager for the soldier's life. With his younger brother, Calvin, and his uncle, Alexander, Morgan enlisted in Oliver P. Beard's company of the First Kentucky Mounted Volunteers (also known as the Kentucky Cavalry) commanded by Colonel Humphrey Marshall. The regiment served longer in that war than any other Kentucky unit - from June 1846 to July 1848. John enlisted as a private, but was elected a second lieutenant before reaching Louisville, where the troops embarked for Memphis. He was promoted to first lieutenant before the regiment reached Mexico.

The Battle of Buena Vista by Carl Nebel

In Mexico Lieutenant John Morgan conducted himself gallantly in the Battle of Buena Vista on February 23, 1847 where the regiment suffered thirty killed-in-action and also thirty wounded-in-action.

The Kentucky Cavalry, along with a regiment of Arkansas Cavalry protected the left flank of the American army. The left wing of the Americans' drew the particular attention of the Mexicans, who tried to turn that flank in violent fighting. The commanding general of the American forces, Major General Zachary Taylor, in his battle report to the Secretary of War, William L. Marcy, particularly mentions that the Kentuckians met the enemy "handsomely."

When his twelve-month enlistment was completed in 1847, Morgan returned to Kentucky. Back in Lexington, he went into business in the woolen industry and also dabbled in the slave trade and hemp production.

In 1848 he married Rebecca Gratz Bruce, the sister of a business partner. They had a stillborn child in 1853.

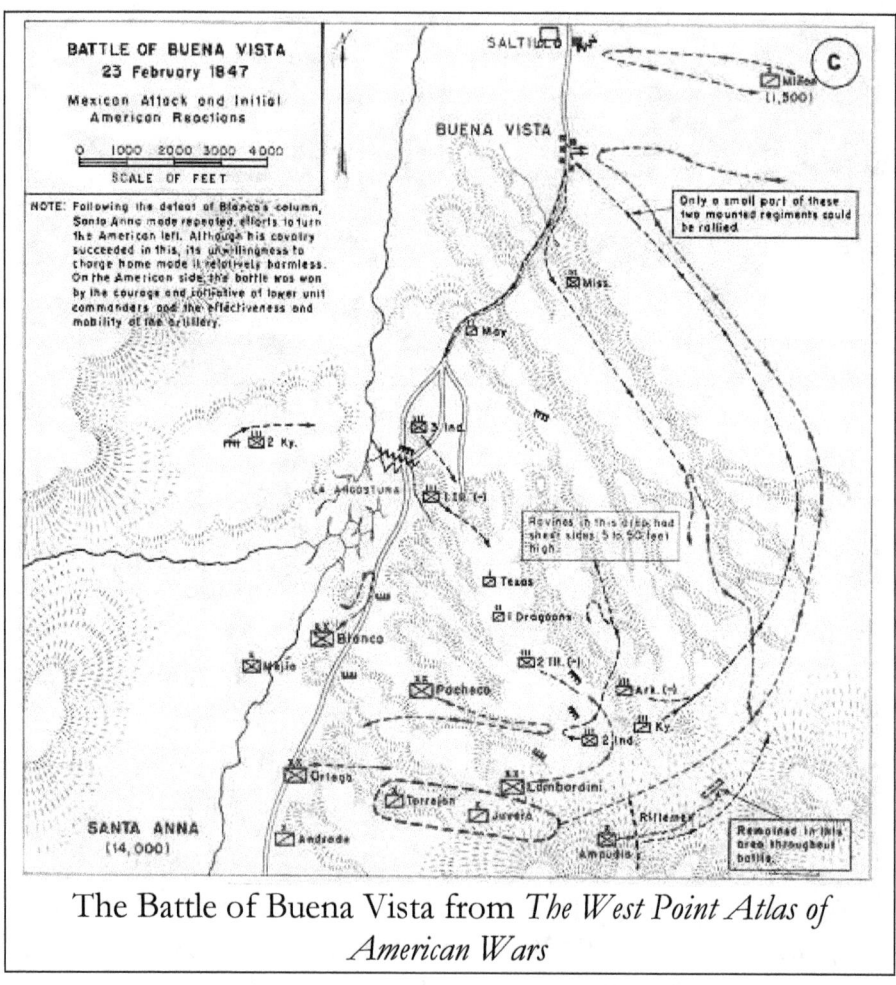

The Battle of Buena Vista from *The West Point Atlas of American Wars*

Rebecca contracted septic thrombophlebitis, an infection of a blood clot in a vein. As a result of this illness one of her legs was amputated and she became an invalid for the remainder of her life. Throughout their marriage, John Morgan was known to be a gambler and "womanizer."

In 1852 Morgan raised a volunteer artillery company. It was disbanded by the state legislature in 1854.

Morgan was very active in Lexington public and social life. He was a member of the Episcopal Church, a Mason, a "Breckenridge Democrat," and the Captain of the Union Volunteer Fire Department.

In 1857, while tensions were growing between North and South, John Morgan organized the Lexington Rifles - an independent infantry company - and became their captain. They were a well-drilled and well-equipped company that attracted considerable attention.

As with most Kentuckians, John Morgan did not initially support secession of the southern states from the Union. In 1860 John wrote to his brother, Thomas Hunt Morgan, a student at Kenyon College in Ohio, his opinion that Abraham Lincoln would be a good President and that secession would be avoided. By the spring, however, Thomas, who agreed with his brother's opinions, had transferred to the Kentucky Military Institute outside of Louisville, Kentucky, and there began to support the Confederacy.

In January 1861, Captain John Hunt Morgan received a communication from the Adjutant General of Kentucky, Simon Bolivar Buckner, asking how many men he could furnish from the Rifles. Morgan answered General Buckner that the Rifles had fifty guns and sixty men.

The Lexington Rifles continued drilling through early 1861 when Unionist and Southerner fought for the support of Kentucky. The state tried to maintain its neutrality.

April 1861 brought the cannonade of Fort Sumter and four days later, on the 16th, Captain Morgan sent the following message to President Jefferson Davis of the Confederate States of America:

> *Twenty thousand men can be raised to defend southern liberty against northern conquest. Do you want them?* (Stoddard, p250)

No answer was received. Perhaps President Davis had too many things on his mind at that date to worry about Kentucky. The Federal Government, however, had time to think about Kentucky, and Camp Robinson was established near Lexington to receive Union recruits, gaining many for the Federalist cause.

On June 8, 1861, Adjutant General Buckner entered into neutrality agreements on behalf of Kentucky with General George B. McClellan for the Union and Governor Isham G. Harris of the state of Tennessee.

General Buckner raised sixty-one companies to defend Kentucky's neutrality in the growing conflict. When the state's neutrality was breached and the board overseeing the state's militia made it impossible for Buckner to perform his duties, the general resigned at accepted a commission in the Confederate Army.

General Buckner went to Tennessee to receive volunteers into the Kentucky State Guard - a unit in the early Confederate Army. Thomas Morgan left Louisville, crossed into Tennessee, and there joined the Kentucky State Guard. John Morgan, however, remained in

Lexington to tend to his failing business, his Lexington Rifles, and his dying wife, Rebecca, who passed away on July 21, 1861.

John Morgan's impatience grew with the tide of the battles, and finally on the night of September 20, 1861, he stole out of Lexington with most of the Lexington Rifles. They went to Bowling Green, Kentucky - the rallying point for the Confederacy in Kentucky.

Battle flag of the Army of Central Kentucky

It was in Bowling Green where the Lexington Rifles, an infantry company, was reorganized into a cavalry unit with three companies (A, B, and C) with Captain John Hunt Morgan still commanding. This reorganization was accomplished on October 27, 1861. A fourth company (D) was added in the spring of 1862.

After a period of training, the "Rifles" were assigned to General William J. Hardee's Corps of the Army of Central Kentucky (C.S.A.), commanded by General Albert Sidney Johnston.

Morgan and his "Rifles" remained a part of General William Hardee's Corps until February 1862, when they were assigned to General John C. Breckinridge's Corps that formed the reserve of the Army of Central Kentucky. As a captain of cavalry the general duty that fell to John Hunt Morgan was scouting. This task occupied him for most of the first year of the war. In these scouting forays he proved very adept and made quite a reputation in daring undertakings of smaller caliber.

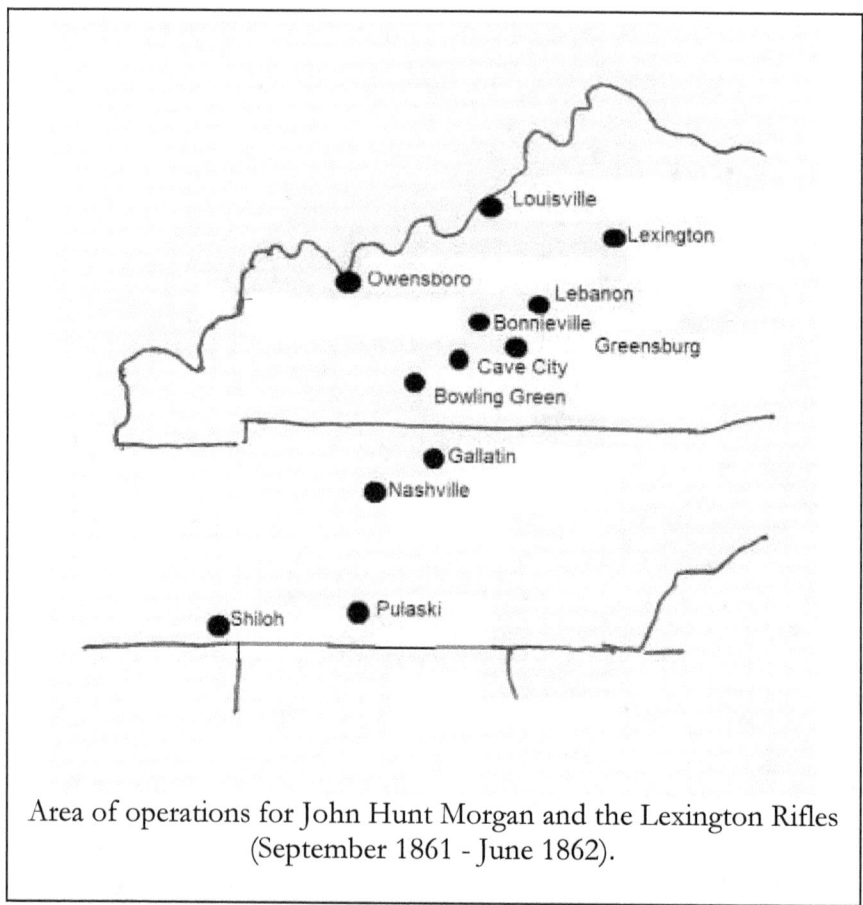

Area of operations for John Hunt Morgan and the Lexington Rifles (September 1861 - June 1862).

Morgan and his "Rifles" began their involvement in the Civil War with an expedition to Bacon Creek Bridge near Bonnieville, Kentucky. The bridge carried the Louisville and Nashville Railroad line across the creek and was an important choke point on an important federal supply line between Bowling Green and Nashville. The bridge had been destroyed in late 1861. Before repairs could be completed, Morgan led the

"Rifles" on a raid - burning the bridge on December 5, 1861, and occupying the area through December 8th. This raid was the public's first introduction to the daring John Hunt Morgan.

From January 28th to February 2nd of the next year, Morgan horsemen were operating around Greensburg and Lebanon, Kentucky. Through the March 8, 1862, they were scouting toward and around Nashville.

Morgan captured the Tennessee town of Gallatin on March 15, 1862, and held it until March 18th. Because of these actions, John Hunt Morgan was promoted to Colonel on April 4, 1862.

WILLIAM WOODROW SLIDER

## 2 SHILOH

In March of 1862 the Army of Central Kentucky (along with Colonel Morgan) was absorbed into the Army of Mississippi. The Army was briefly commanded by General P.T.G Beauregard and then General A.S. Johnston, who led the Army into the Battle of Shiloh. Morgan and his cavalrymen were assigned to the Army of Mississippi as an independent regiment.

The Battle of Shiloh is significant in the brief military career of John Morgan, because it is the largest engagement in which he led troops. It must have had a profound impact on his development as a combat leader. It is helpful, therefore, to examine this battle in some detail.

By April 5, 1862, General U.S. Grant had landed five of the six divisions of the Army of the Tennessee (35,000 men) at Pittsburg Landing. The sixth division under the command of General Lew Wallace (also known as the author of the novel, *Ben Hur*) had been left five miles down stream (north) to secure Crump's Landing. Grant himself established his headquarters nine miles downstream from his army's encampment.

The union divisions, encamped in the triangular area that would become the battlefield around Shiloh Church, were located wherever the soldiers could find suitable clearings. The ground, except for a few cleared areas and some roadways, was covered with forest and undergrowth and dissected by waterways. It was difficult terrain for cavalry. Inexplicably, no plans had been made for the defense of the Shiloh Church area.

By the evening of April 5th, the Confederate troops (numbering 45,000) had advanced unobserved to within two miles of the Union's lead elements. The southerners camped in the order of battle in which they would attack the next day - Hardee's III Corps (reinforced by one of Bragg's brigades) in the lead in a two-mile-long line, followed by General Braxton Bragg's II Corps, also in-line; then I Corps of General Leonidas Polk, who was also the Episcopal Bishop of Louisiana; followed by Breckinridge's Reserve Corps in marching order.

At about 6:00am on the morning of April 6th, Johnston's army moved forward against an ill-prepared enemy. The lead Northern units were General Benjamin Prentiss' division in the center; General William T. Sherman's division (minus) on the right flank around Shiloh Church; and General Alexander Stuart's brigade of Sherman's division on the left flank.

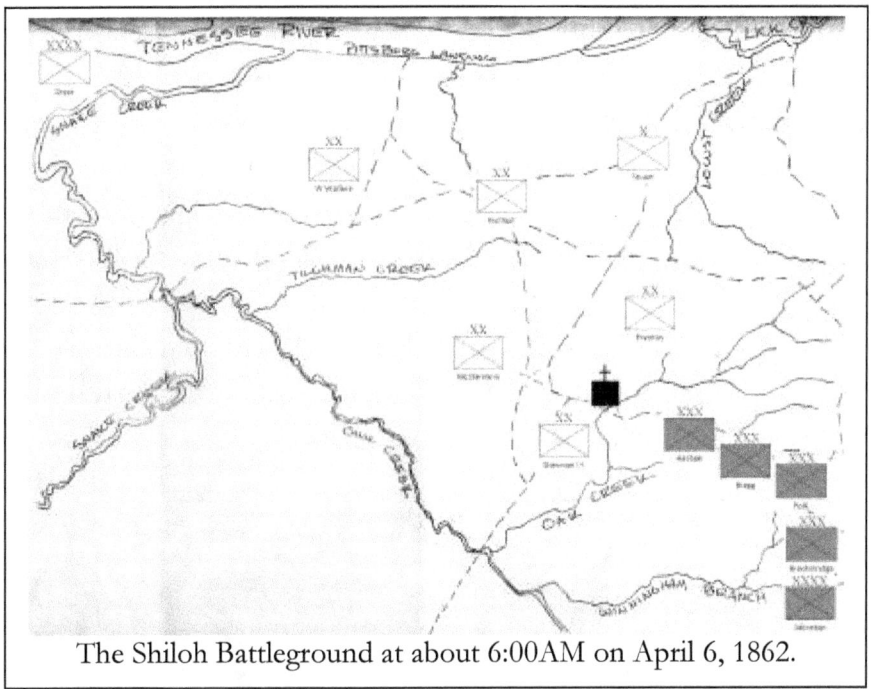
The Shiloh Battleground at about 6:00AM on April 6, 1862.

The Confederate plan was to make the main effort against Grant's left flank that was anchored on the Tennessee River, driving them against the Snake and Owl Creeks, and separating them of their line of communication and supply. The Confederate formation, however, did not concentrate enough forces against Grant's left and III Corps and II Corps became entangled all along the front.

At 7:30am, General Beauregard (Johnston's deputy commander) ordered I Corps and the Reserve Corps into the battle, simply extending the line. The attack devolved into a large uncoordinated frontal assault all along the front, seeking to envelop both Union flanks.

The Union forces were functioning somewhat better in the defensive despite the absence of their commanding general from the battlefield. Divisional commanders were coordinating and communicating very well.

By 9:00am, however, Sherman's division (minus) had broken, but at Sherman's request General John A. McClernand's division came forward and stabilized the line. Prentiss' division, likewise, was supported by General Stephen A. Hurlbut's division.

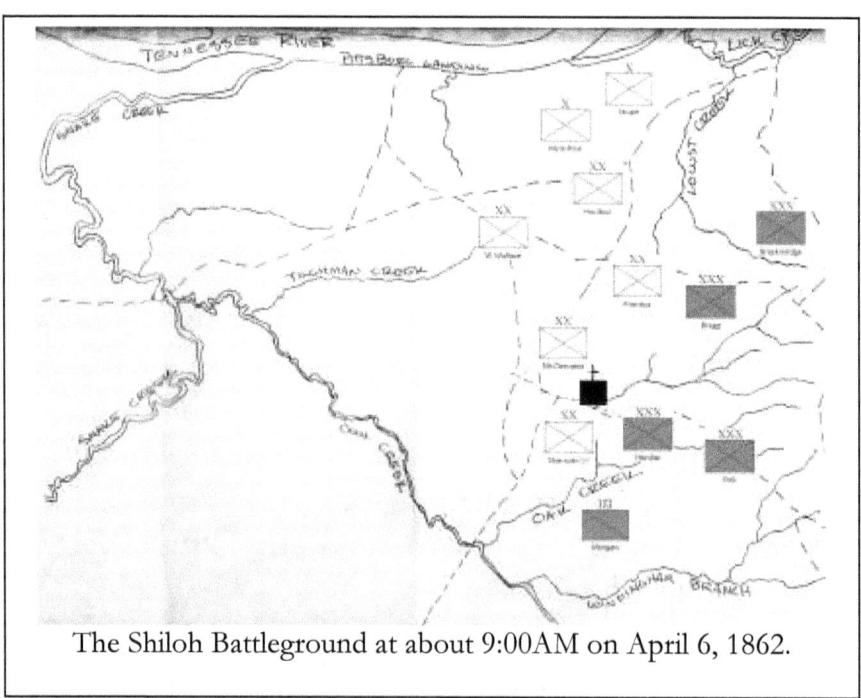

The Shiloh Battleground at about 9:00AM on April 6, 1862.

By this time, Grant had arrived on the scene. He directed General William Wallace to establish a line of defense behind the battle and secure the Snake Creek bridge. Grant also sent word to General Lew Wallace to bring his division to the battle.

Where was Colonel Morgan's cavalry during the initial phase of the battle? The Lexington Rifles were more than likely located on the left flank of the Confederates opposite Sherman's division. They would not have been in the thick of the battle, but certainly would be screening the advancing Confederate flank, threatening the Union flank, and developing routes for continuing the advance.

It seems that during the morning of April 5th Grant's intention was to stabilize a line that would protect the Pittsburg Landing and the bridge at the junction of the Snake and Owl Creeks so that reinforcements could arrive.

By mid-day the Confederate soldiers were reaching the point of exhaustion. They had slept in formation the night before and had scant rations. As the Southerners advanced, many dropped out in order to consume the ample abandoned Union rations. Sherman and McClernand continued to be forced back through the afternoon, but were able to inflict heavy casualties on Hardee's III Corps.

At about 4:00pm on April 6th, II Corps (Bragg) and the Reserve Corps (Breckinridge) accomplished the original intent of the Confederate attack - to envelop the Union left flank, as Hurlbut's division began to crumble.

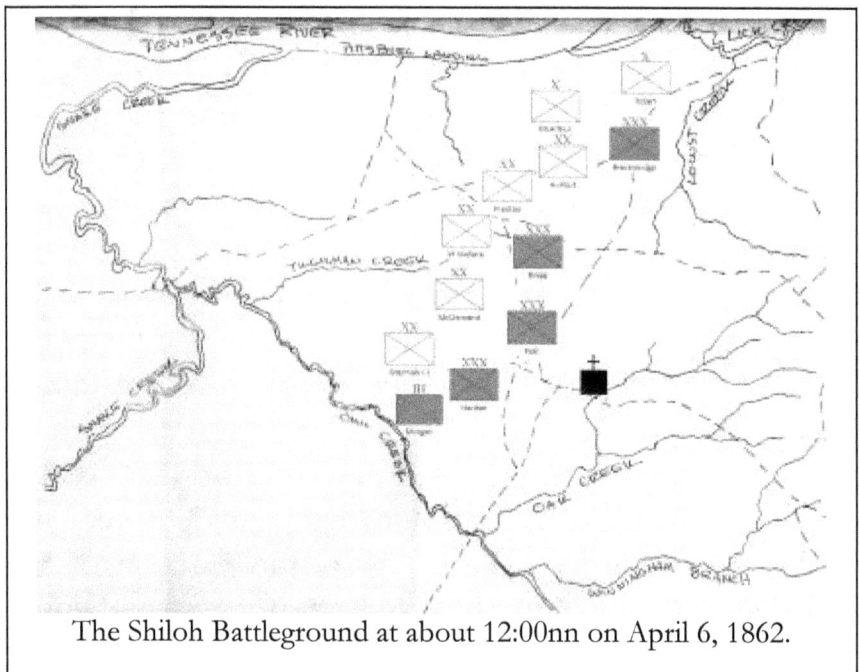

The Shiloh Battleground at about 12:00nn on April 6, 1862.

The Union divisions of Prentiss and William Wallace, however, had remained steady for the last five hours. These divisions withstood twelve separate attacks and constant artillery fire. General Johnston himself was leading an attack on these positions when he was mortally wounded. General Beauregard assumed command of the Army of the Mississippi.

Shortly after 4:00pm Sherman and McClernand began to withdraw their divisions to prepared positions east of Tilghman Creek. They joined McArthur's brigade that was protecting the main north/south roadway.

On the opposite Union flank along the Tennessee River, Stuart withdrew his brigade to Pittsburg Landing, thereby exposing Hurlbut's division. This action in turn caused Hurlbut to withdraw, leaving the divisions of

William Wallace and Prentiss exposed and isolated. The Union left was collapsing.

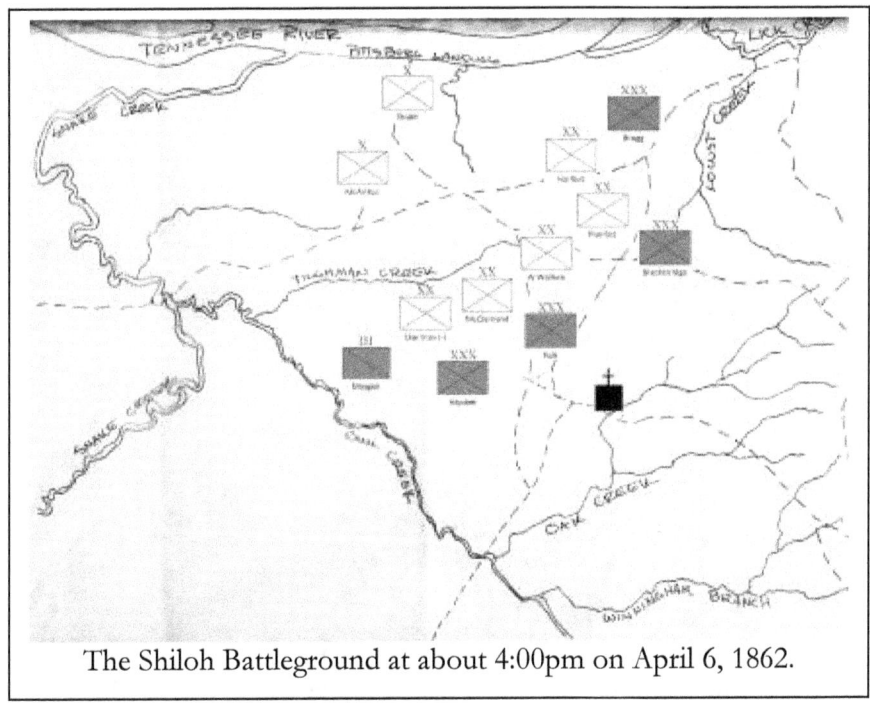

The Shiloh Battleground at about 4:00pm on April 6, 1862.

William Wallace tried to extricate his division from the trap by simply turning his troops and marching toward the other withdrawn units. Two of his regiments were able to escape, but their commander fell, mortally wounded.

Prentiss circled his division and the remaining regiment of Wallace's division. They were quickly surrounded by Breckinridge and Polk's two corps. After gallant resistance, Prentiss surrendered around 5:30pm.

As Prentiss' division was collapsing, Hardee's III Corps and Bragg's II Corps were able to sweep forward to threaten the Union left that was anchored on the

Tennessee River at Pittsburg Landing. The South's left flank continued to be covered by the army's cavalry - including Colonel Morgan's "Lexington Rifles."

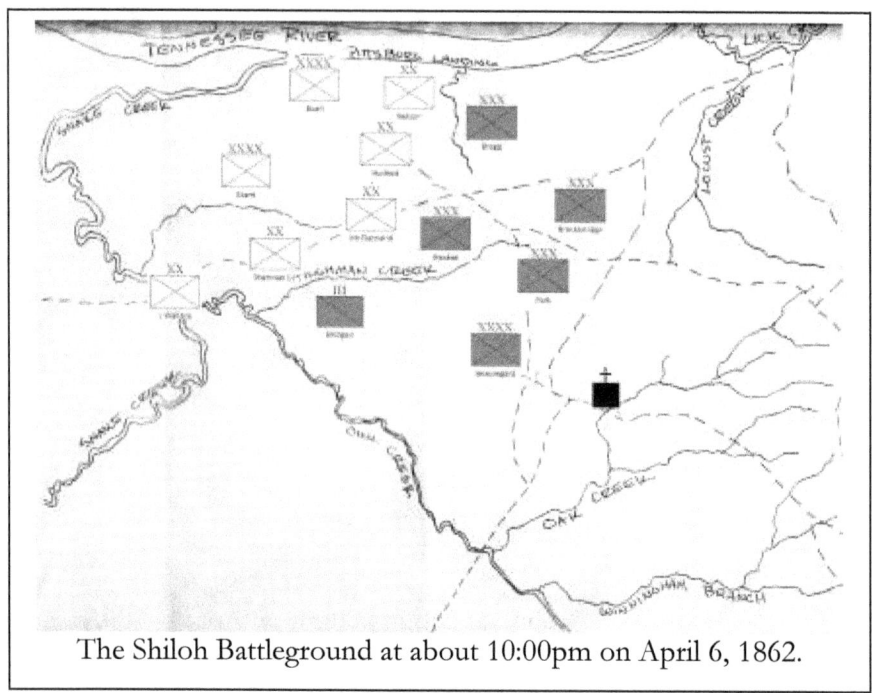

The Shiloh Battleground at about 10:00pm on April 6, 1862.

By the end of the day - April 6th - Grant had stabilized his Army of the Tennessee, but a great cost. General Lew Wallace's division finally arrived on Sherman's right flank - probably opposite Morgan - having taken some precious time trying to locate the Union positions. In the confusion of the battle, the general had literally marched his division in full circle in order to reverse direction. Grant was not pleased with the delay.

All was not lost for the Union, however. Late in the afternoon of April 6th, the lead division of General Don Carlos Buell's Army of the Ohio (30,000) began arriving.

This lead division, under General William "Bull" Nelson - a former Naval officer - was crossing the Tennessee River. Union gunboats also began firing into the Confederate's right flank.

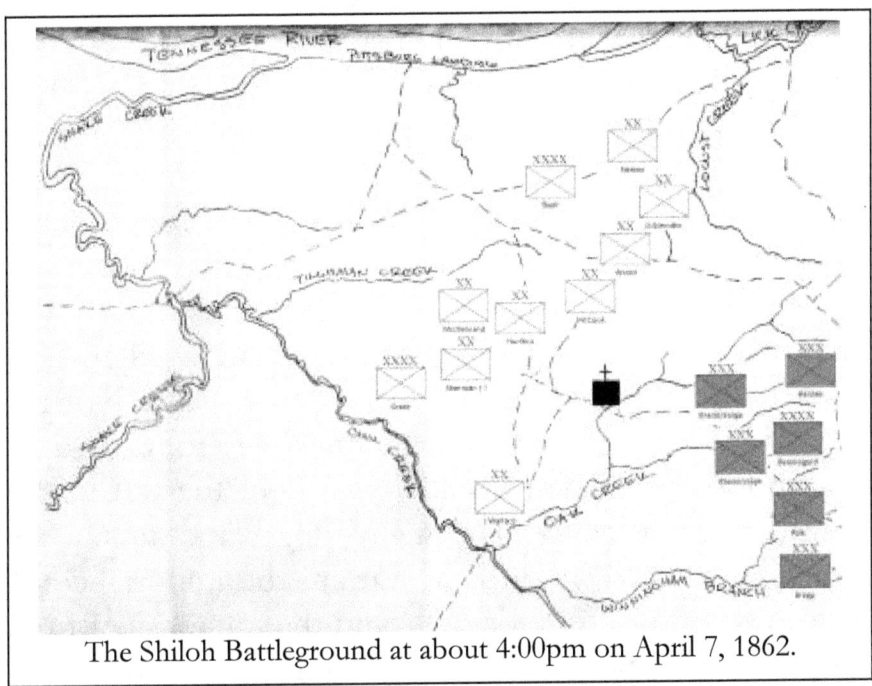

The Shiloh Battleground at about 4:00pm on April 7, 1862.

The stormy and rainy night gave both sides an opportunity to rest. The next morning would bring the battle to a conclusion.

The two union armies - Grant on the right and Buell on the left - began their counterattack at sunrise. Reinvigorated by the reinforcements, the Northerners began to push the depleted Southerners back.

General Beauregard issued the orders for retreat at about 2:30pm. By 4:00pm the Confederates had withdrawn behind Breckenridge's covering force.

Once the Union armies reached their original encampments from April 5th, their aggressive attack slowed. The Confederates were allowed to escape under the screen of their cavalry back to Corinth, and the Federals were left in possession of the battlefield.

The battle was a costly one. Union forces lost about 14,000 men killed, wounded, and missing. The Confederates lost about 11,000 (*The West Point Atlas of American Wars*, vol. 1).

Though Colonel John Hunt Morgan would have played a peripheral role in the Battle of Shiloh and would not have been engaged in the heavy fighting of the infantry, still the battle would have had a significant impact on his views of conducting war. The North's capacity to concentrate large numbers of troops and to absorb losses, the North's ability to fight the war in the South, the difficulty in maneuvering large units, the confusion caused by difficult terrain, the importance of waterways and water crossings, and the immensity of the losses on both sides would have led him to see the value - and even necessity - of the South adopting a strategy of lightning strikes designed to harass and incapacity enemy units and to demoralize the civilian populous. One could argue that out of his experience at Shiloh, John Hunt Morgan developed a more effective - a possibly a more humane - means for the South to take the battle to the enemy.

## 3 STONES RIVER

In the spring and summer of 1862, Morgan set out on independent raids to harass the North. During the rest of April and May of 1862 he operated in middle Tennessee. In June of 1862 the "Lexington Rifles" and other remnants of cavalry remaining from the Battle of Shiloh were reorganized into the 2nd Cavalry Regiment, of the Army of Mississippi, CSA.

The Army of Mississippi following the Battle of Shiloh had several commanding generals. P.G.T Beauregard assumed command of the army during the Battle of Shiloh when General A.S. Johnston was mortally wounded on April 6th. Beauregard relinquished command to General Braxton Bragg on May 6th. General William Hardee assumed temporary command on July 5th until August 15th, when Bragg returned to command of the army. On September 28th General Leonidas Polk ("The Fighting Bishop") assumed temporary command and led the army in the Battle of Perryville. Bragg relieved Polk on November 7th and retained command until this particular version of the Army of Mississippi was renamed the Army of Tennessee on November 20th. Bragg was commanding general of the new Army of Tennessee for the remainder of 1862.

*Editor's note: The reader will notice from the chronology above, that formations and commanders in during the Civil War were very fluid and challenging to trace. The essential understanding for the reader is that from the end of the Battle of Shiloh and through the end of 1862 John Hunt Morgan led an independent cavalry unit under the oversight and in support of General Braxton Bragg's army.*

Beginning in July of 1862 Bragg began to position his Army of Mississippi (later Tennessee) for a cooperative effort with General Kirby Smith's Army of East Tennessee - an invasion of Kentucky. Bragg used two of his cavalry units - General Nathan B. Forrest's brigade and Colonel Morgan's regiment - to disrupt the enemy and deprive them of needed supplies in support of the planned invasion of Kentucky. Bragg employed Morgan's Raiders for deep penetrations into enemy territory independent of the army's senior cavalry commander - General Forrest. In July 1862, while Bragg was consolidating his force in Chattanooga near Smith's in Knoxville, he sent Forrest against the Union forces in Murfreesboro, while he sent Morgan far northward into Kentucky.

Morgan and his "Raiders" entered Kentucky on several occasions. The three most significant raids were the First Kentucky Raid, the Christmas Raid, and the Great Raid. Morgan's raids were designed to create a diversion and to cover Bragg's army (Henry, p296).

Morgan's chief-of-staff and brother-in-law, Basil Duke, indicates that Bragg ordered Morgan to go any place in Kentucky and then return for the inevitable showdown. Morgan, however, insisted on the authority to plunge into enemy territory. Morgan felt that a raid into Kentucky alone would soon be forced back and result only in a temporary respite for the Confederate armies in Tennessee. Morgan was convinced that a drive into the enemy's country would draw large bodies of troops in pursuit of him and weaken the forces opposing Bragg.

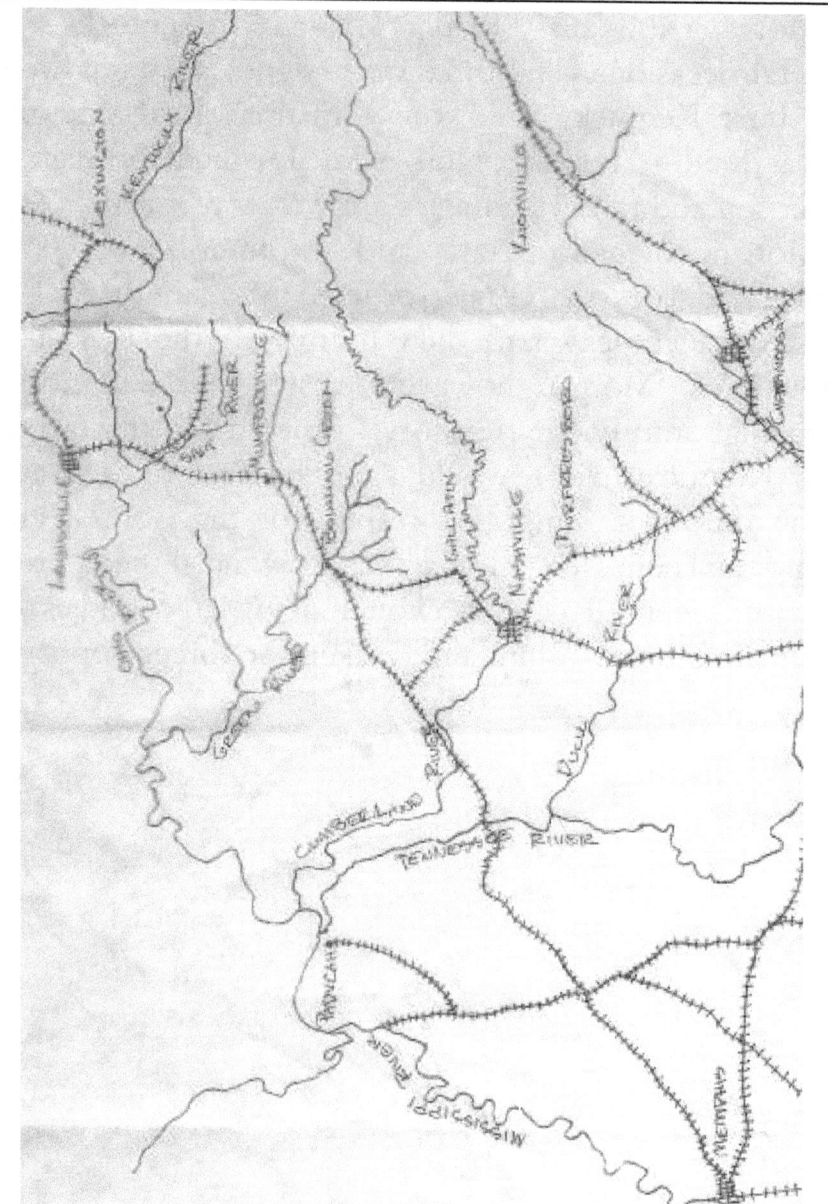

Area of Operations for the Army of Mississippi (later Tennessee) and the Army of East Tennessee during 1862 without state boundaries. The map is in this format in order to show the tactical insignificance of state boundaries and the strategic and tactical significance of waterways, railways, and water crossings. Rivers and railroads provided lines of strategic communications and mobility for both Armies. Railroad bridges over rivers were critical chokepoints. The importance of rivers is illustrated by the North's practice of naming its armies after the major rivers where they operated.

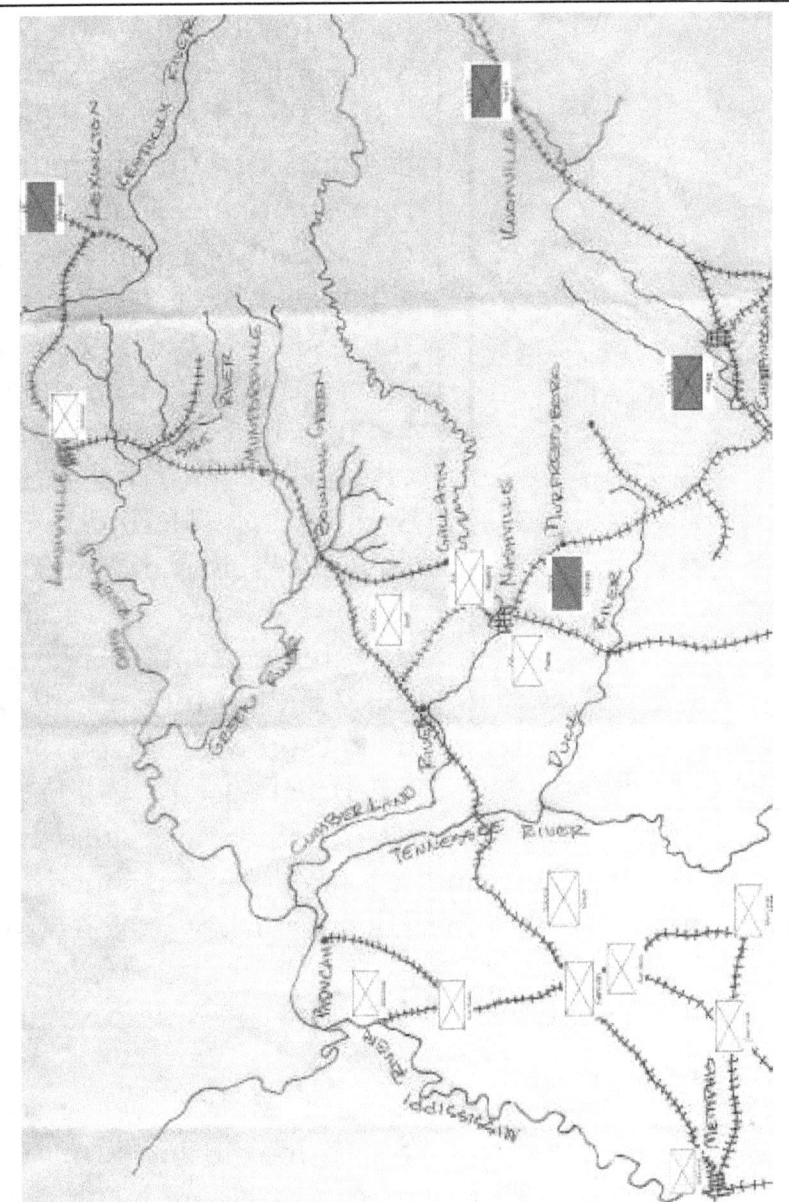

The beginning of the Stones River Campaign in July 1862 - Bragg had withdrawn his army from Tupelo, Mississippi - leaving reinforced divisions to fix Grant's army - and repositioned his force by railroad through Mobile, Alabama, to Chattanooga, Tennessee. General Kirby Smith's army was located at Knoxville. Bragg continued to harass and slow the movement of Buell's army with a raid from his army's cavalry corps commanded General Nathanael Forrest at Murfreesboro, and with the far reaching raid by Morgan who reached far into Northern Kentucky.

Morgan's Raid of July 1862
(from TrailsRUs.com)

On July 8, 1862 Colonel Morgan led the 2nd Cavalry on its First Kentucky Raid in hopes of bringing much support to the South. He crossed into Kentucky at Tompkinsville and surprised the Union garrison there. From there he marched northward to Glasgow, Lebanon, Springfield, Harrodsburg, Lawrenceburg, and finally turned back to escape capture at Cynthiana. In this raid, Morgan's 900 men captured and paroled 1,200 Federal soldiers, destroyed massive quantities of supplies, and acquired several hundred horses. The success of the raid was a key reason why Generals Bragg and Smith launched the Confederate Heartland Offensive of 1862 - known as the Stones River Campaign.

In August Morgan was back in Middle Tennessee raiding Union forces there. Smith moved his Army of East Tennessee from Knoxville to Lexington, Kentucky. Bragg's Army of Mississippi remained in Chattanooga until August 28th.

Buell's advance toward Chattanooga was slowed in July by damage to the Nashville and Chattanooga Railroad, but when the line was repaired he continued the advance. He sent divisions to guard chokepoints between Nashville and Chattanooga. His lead divisions by the end of August were within forty miles of Bragg in Chattanooga.

Grant's army remained in western Kentucky and Tennessee. They guarded railroad junctions and bridges.

On August 12, Colonel Morgan led his cavalry regiment into Union occupied territory to Gallatin, Tennessee - about thirty miles northeast of Nashville. There his force disrupted communications and supplies by destroying a railroad tunnel. Buell was unable to respond because he lacked the cavalry to match the Southern horsemen. Also, the infantry units could not intercept the raiders. In addition, isolated garrisons had poor discipline and security and were easy targets for fast-riding and disciplined raiding parties.

In eastern Tennessee General Kirby Smith began his advance northward in mid-August. He arrived in Lexington with his army on August 30th. Smith sent advance parties to Harrodsburg, Frankfort, and northern Kentucky. Both Louisville and Cincinnati were garrisoned by large numbers of Union troops, but these were newly recruited and untrained soldiers.

When he received word that Kirby Smith was nearing Lexington, General Bragg left Chattanooga (August 28th). Initially, Bragg's advance was hidden from Buell by poor scouting by the Union cavalry. Bragg advanced behind the plateau of the Cumberland Mountains and Buell halted his advanced - confused about Bragg's intention.

The intent of the Southern commanders - Smith and Bragg - was to fix Grant with small units in northern

Mississippi, to cooperate in an invasion of Kentucky, and to cut Buell's line of communication and supply to Louisville. Buell would be defeated and then the two armies would turn on Grant in the west. The Confederate offensive had started.

Through September the tactical situation changed significantly. Kirby Smith's Army of East Tennessee was firmly established in Lexington and threatening Louisville and Cincinnati, both of which were garrisoned by large numbers of new recruits. Bragg's Army of Mississippi advanced northward and traveled through Glasgow, Kentucky to reach Munfordville by the end of the month.

On the Union side Grant's Army of the Mississippi remained dispersed throughout western Kentucky and Tennessee. After Bragg's rapid advance, Buell was slow in deciding what to do with his Army of the Ohio. Eventually, he decided on a rapid withdrawal northward, paralleling Bragg's advance. By the end of September, Buell had consolidated his army in Bowling Green, Kentucky, with Bragg sitting astride the railroad line in Munfordville - blocking Buell's line of communication and supply.

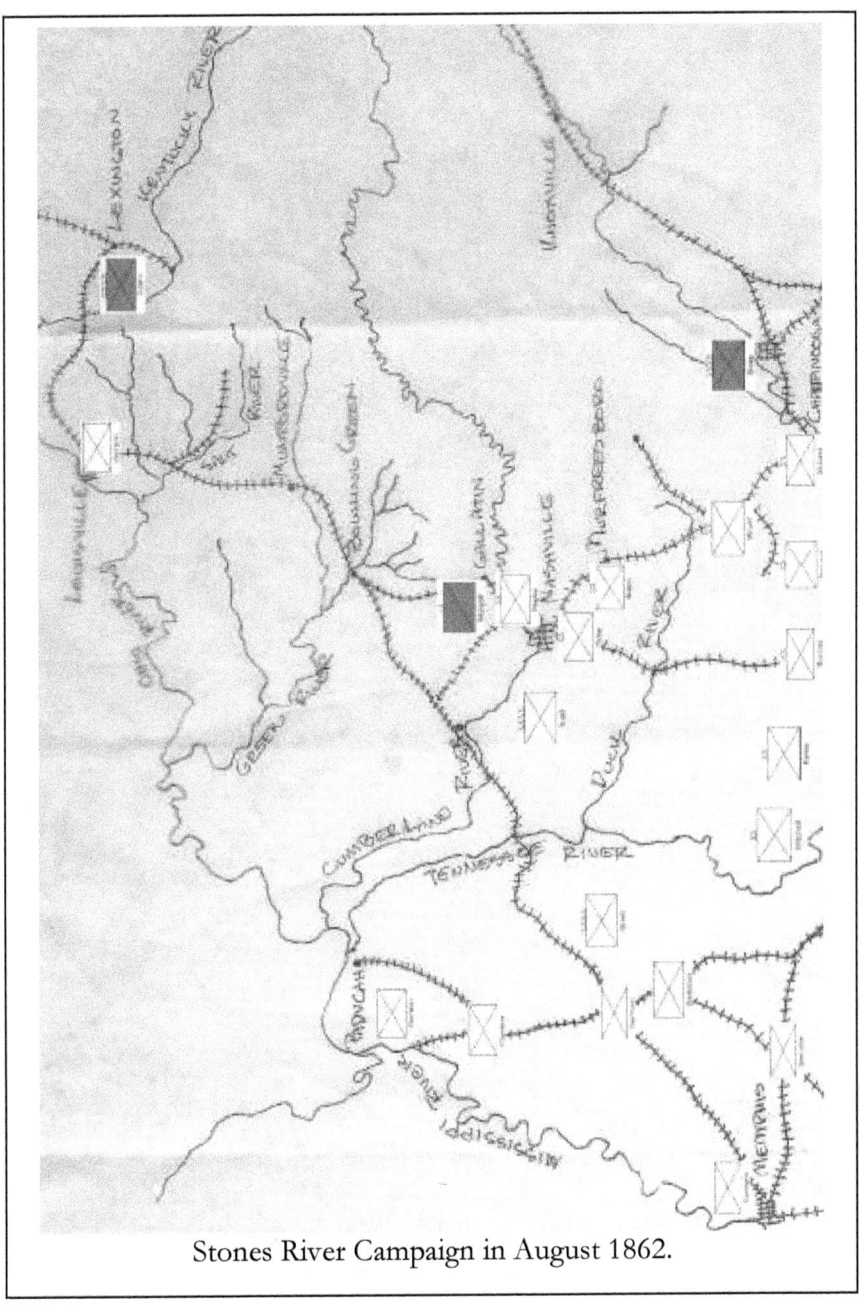

Stones River Campaign in August 1862.

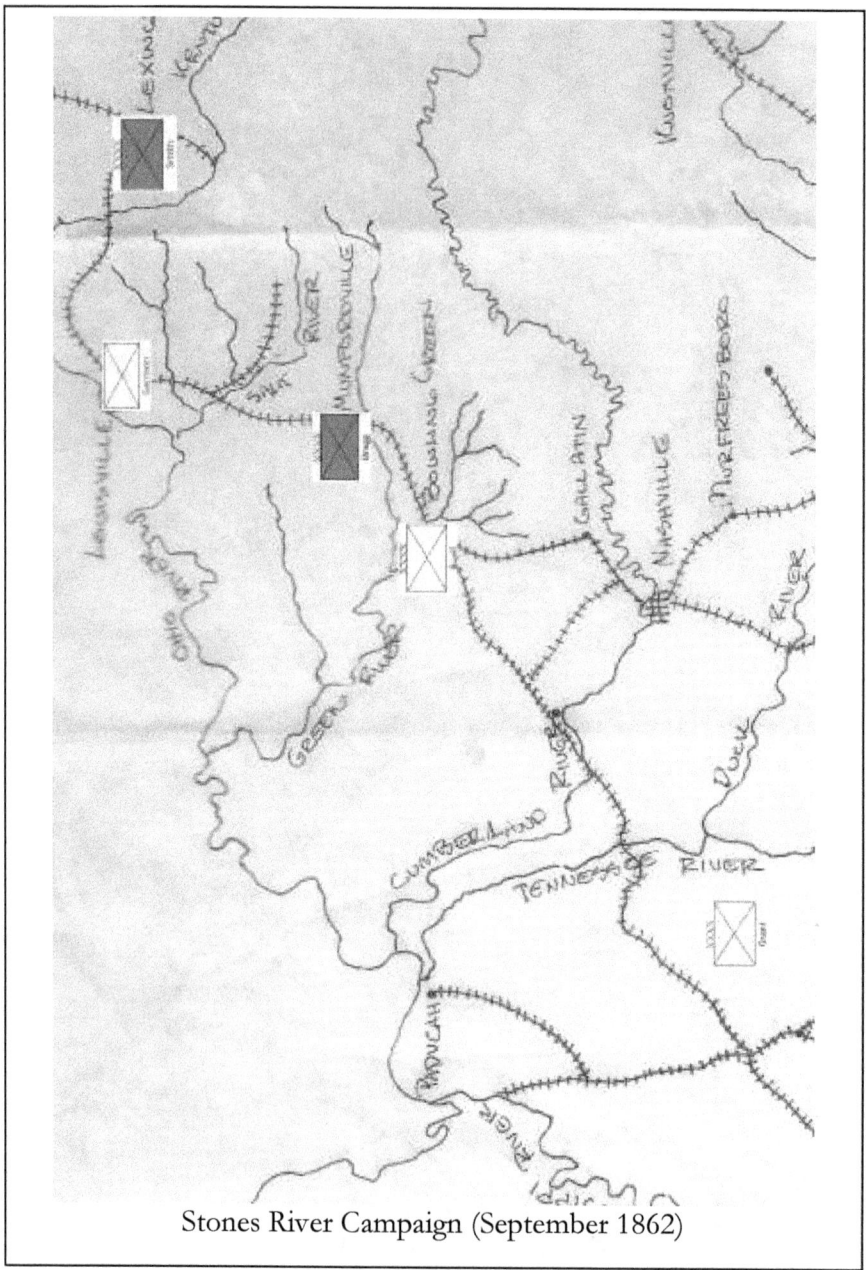
Stones River Campaign (September 1862)

Bragg was reluctant to attack Buell because he felt that Buell's force was much larger than his. Instead of attacking, Buell advanced northward to Bardstown - about forty miles from Louisville. Buell then withdrew to Louisville.

On October 1, 1862, knowing that the Federal government was dissatisfied with his leadership, Buell began marching southward. On October 7th he located Bragg's army at Perryville, Kentucky. Fighting began in the morning of October 8th.

Realizing that he was facing Buell's entire army, Bragg ordered a withdrawal to Harrodsburg. He was joined there by Kirby Smith on October 10th.

Apparently Bragg believed that the offensive had failed. He retreated through the Cumberland Gap to Chattanooga and then to Murfreesboro.

Buell was relieved of command in October. His superiors were disappointed in his lackluster and timid leadership. General William Rosecrans took command of the newly named Army of the Cumberland.

In November, Kirby Smith's Army of the East Tennessee was absorbed into the Army of Tennessee as III Corps. Smith was eventually transferred to a command in the west.

Bragg and his Army of Tennessee now faced two excellent commanders and their armies - Grant and the Army of the Mississippi, and Rosecrans and the Army of the Cumberland - and two excellent commanders (Grant and Rosecrans). Bragg, however, possessed one great asset - his cavalry units commanded by General Nathan Bedford Forrest, General Joseph Wheeler, and Colonel John Hunt Morgan. Soon Bragg would unleash Forrest on Grant and Morgan on Rosecrans.

In early December General Bragg ordered Colonel Morgan to move northward and operate along Rosencrans' lines of communication and supply. Rosecrans had begun to move his army from Nashville toward Murfreesboro. Leaving Baird's Mill in southern Wilson County, Tennessee on the morning of December 6th, Morgan's troops went forward.

After being allowed to select two regiments of Infantry - the 2nd Kentucky and 11th Kentucky - containing some 700 men from Col. Roger W. Hanson's "Kentucky Brigade" - Morgan chose the 2nd and 9th Kentucky Cavalry commanded by his uncle, Col. Thomas H. Hunt, as well as an artillery battery. His own men consisted of the 7th, 8th, 11th Kentucky Cavalry Regiments and a group of local men commanded by Hartsville's Col. James D. Bennett - the 9th Tennessee Cavalry. Morgan's brother-in-law, Col. Basil W. Duke, was in overall command of the cavalry along with two of Morgan's own Kentucky artillery batteries.

With the officers only knowing their destination, many rumors began to fly among the enlisted men. After arriving in Lebanon in the early afternoon and marching in sleet and snow for eight miles, Morgan stopped his men to rest and eat. As they left Lebanon they were told of their destination - Hartsville. Jubilation went throughout the ranks as they continued their long march toward Hartsville - seventeen miles away.

On December 7th Morgan reached Hartsville. Colonel Morgan was always warmly received by the citizens of Hartsville, but this time the warmth of his reception would be increased by 39th Infantry Brigade of the Union Army.

The Union brigade was commanded by Colonel Absalom B. Moore and consisted of the 106th and 108th Ohio Infantry Regiments, the 104th Illinois Infantry Regiment, the 13th Indiana Artillery Regiment, the 2nd Indiana Cavalry Regiment, and a detachment of the 11th Kentucky Calvary Regiment of the Union Army.

Arriving at the Cumberland River at 10:00pm, Morgan's expeditionary force began their crossing of the cold dark water. Taking longer than expected to cross the swollen Cumberland, Colonel Morgan, the infantry, artillery, and a small part of the cavalry crossed at Puryears Bend. Colonel Duke with the majority of the cavalry, crossed a few miles farther down river.

Hurrying to meet Morgan at their planned rendezvous point, Duke left a large portion of his men on the south side of the river. With daylight breaking and the surprise element almost gone, the Duke set out with out the rest of the cavalry units, who were still crossing the river. Colonel Bennett and his 9th Tennessee Cavalry were sent into town to cut off any escape the Federals might take.

Because of the complicated river crossing, Morgan's force was now reduced to 1,300. As they approached the Federal camp, the first Union pickets were captured, but their backups fired shots at the fast wheeling Confederates and prevented their surprise attack. The cry was heard, "The Rebels are coming!"

Soon it became apparent by the many campfires that the Union numbers were much greater than at first anticipated. Colonel Duke exclaimed to Morgan, "You have more work cut out for you than you bargained for."

Morgan answered, "Yes, and you gentlemen must whip and catch these fellows, and cross the river in two hours and a half, or we'll have six thousand more on our backs."

Doing just that, Morgan's men, in one hour and fifteen minutes, out-maneuvered and out-fought the enemy - totally defeating a much larger force than their own. Federal losses were fifty-eight killed, 204 wounded, and 1,834 captured; total lost were 2,096. Southern losses were twenty-one killed, 104 wounded, and fourteen missing for a total of 139.

Having to hurry to re-cross the Cumberland for the second time in less than nine hours, Colonel Morgan did what most thought could not be done. He successfully transported his men and prisoners back across the chilly water before the Federal reinforcements at Castalian Springs could arrive.

Arriving back in Murfreesboro with their captured wagons, arms, and much needed supplies, Morgan and his men were received and honored by the many local citizens along the route as they returned triumphantly as heroes. The victory was a much-needed boost to the morale of the Confederates.

Morgan was highly praised by all for this most brilliant achievement and the Confederate Congress congratulated him. Confederate President Jefferson Davis arrived on December 11th to promote Morgan to the rank of Brigadier General. Morgan was thirty-seven years old.

General Hardee had urged President Davis to commission Morgan a Major General instead of a Brigadier General. Davis, however, demurred. "I do not wish," the President said, "to give my boys all t plums at once." (Duke, p317)

General Bragg complimented the entire comm ̱ and ordered that the name *"Hartsville"* be inscribed on the banners of all regiments participating. (hartsvilletrousdale.com, civilwaralbum.com, americancivilwar.com)

Three days later, Morgan took some much needed personal time and married Martha "Mattie" Ready. His honeymoon would not last long, however.

Before Christmas of 1862, Bragg ordered two of his cavalry commanders - General Forrest and General Morgan deep into enemy territory. This order would remove both commanders and their forces from the concluding battle of the Stones River Campaign - the Battle of Murfreesboro. Though absent from the battle, both Forrest and Morgan would continue to grow in stature and reputation as military commanders through their conduct of their respective operations.

The culminating battle of the Stones River Campaign was fought astride the Stones River and Murfreesboro, Tennessee. The Confederate Army of Tennessee with 35,000 men under Bragg was established in defensive positions around Murfreesboro, and the Federal Army of the Cumberland with 41,000 men under Rosecrans was located in Nashville - about 35 miles northwest.

Rosecrans left Nashville on December 26th. The two armies met on December 31st in what has been called the Battle of Stones River or the Second Battle of Murfreesboro. Since Morgan was not directly involved in the Second Battle of Murfreesboro, it will only be presented briefly.

The reader may envision the battle field as the face of a clock with the city of Murfreesboro in the center and north at twelve o'clock. The face of the clock is about six miles in diameter.

The west fork of the Stones River flows northward toward Murfreesboro from six o'clock and then turns at the city and flows from Murfreesboro toward eleven o'clock. The river does not follow a straight path, but meanders violently through the countryside. Above Murfreesboro are a group of hills and heights east of the river in narrow fan from eleven o'clock to twelve o'clock. Rosecrans approached Murfreesboro from the northwest from about ten on the clock's face.

Bragg made a strange disposition of the two corps that he had to face Rosecrans. For some reason (some suggest that he wished to avoid any damage to the city of Murfreesboro) he placed most of his army west of the river. Hardee's corps (minus Breckinridge's division) had the Confederate left flank at nine o'clock; Polk's full corps was the center of the line at ten and eleven o'clock - also west of the river. Polk's corps in part was dissected by a meander in the river that limited communication and maneuver in his rear. On the east side of the river above the city at twelve o'clock occupying the hills was Breckinridge's division of Hardee's corps. Rosecrans initially remained on the west side of the river with General Thomas Crittenden's corps on his left (northern) flank facing Polk; General Alexander McCook's corps on the Union right facing Hardee; and General George Thomas' corps in reserve.

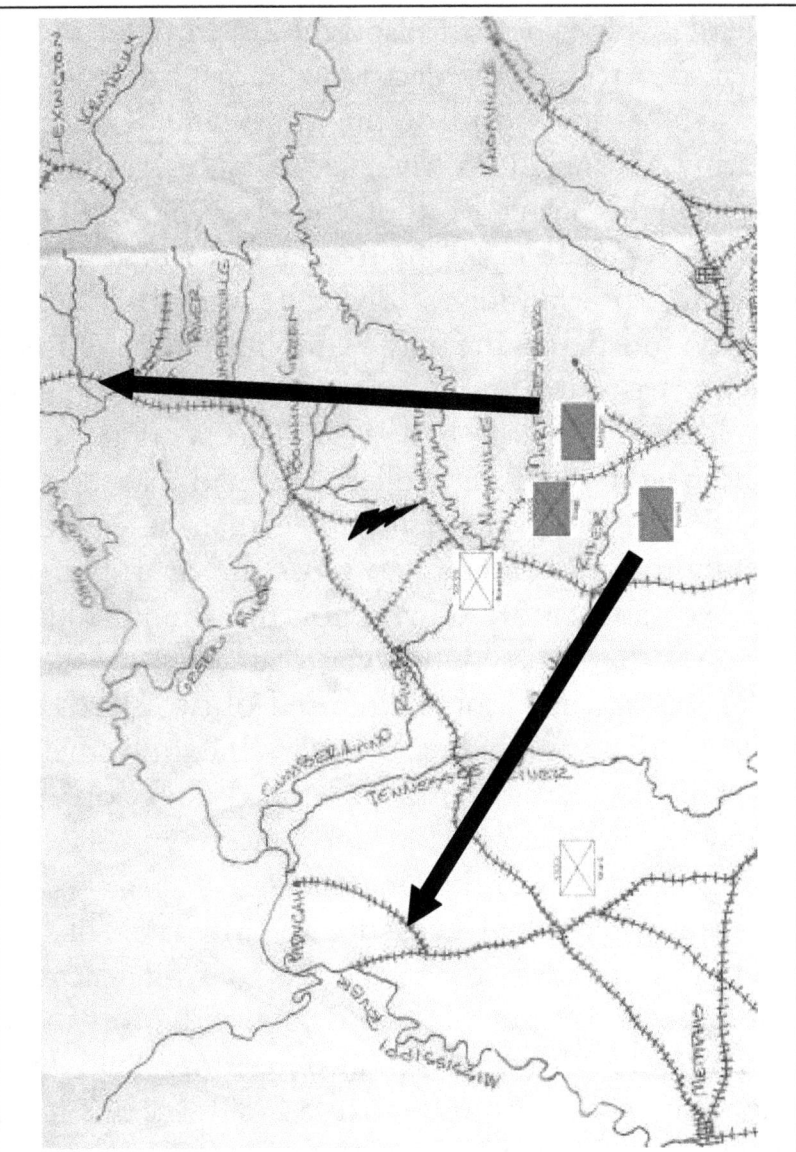

Stones River Campaign (December 1862) showing Confederate cavalry raids and general concentrations of armies. Grant's army was spread throughout western Tennessee and Kentucky.

Bragg made significant errors that probably cost him the battle. First, he had disposed his army on the west side of the river. This decision removed the river as a defensive barrier and made the only route of retreat for his army to include a river crossing. If Bragg had positioned his army west of the river he would have force Rosecrans to cross the river in order to attack him.

Second, Breckinridge's division was place on the elevation north of the city with his flank refused or bending eastward away from the enemy to avoid encirclement. If Bragg had placed Breckenridge squarely on the heights with his artillery and had placed his two corps on the west side of the river, then he would have not only forced Rosecrans to cross the river, but would have been able to fire down upon the Union soldiers in enfilade as they crossed the river to attack.

Third, Bragg had stripped himself of two-thirds of the cavalry. He was all but blind to the movements of Rosecrans. As the battle developed the Confederate generals showed confusion and uncertainty as to the intent and location of the Union army.

Fourth, Bragg had turned loose two of his three cavalry commanders to harass the to Union armies in Tennessee and Kentucky. Forrest and Morgan took their mounted forces deep into territory held by the Union, but too far from the battle for Rosecrans to have any immediate concern about them.

Fifth, uncharacteristic of most Confederate generals, Bragg allowed his adversary to strike first. It is a strange quirk of battle that the first shot usually wins. It is a strange quirk of this particular battle that both opposing armies had essentially the same plan - to turn the enemy's right flank and then force them onto the river. Rosecrans won because he struck first and took the initiative away from Bragg.

Still, Bragg could have won the battle, and it looked as if he would.  In the end, however, Rosecrans was rescued by a much-needed supply train, and Bragg was unable to dislodge the Federals.

The ending was similar to Shiloh.  The Confederates retreated southward, and Union forces failed to pursue.  The North had lost more men, but remained in control of the battlefield (*The West Point Atlas of American Wars*, vol. 1).

Where was Morgan?  On December 22nd Bragg had unleashed Morgan's brigade to harass Rosecrans' rear.  Morgan's drive northward became known as the Christmas Raid.

The Second Battle of Murfreesboro

# WILLIAM WOODROW SLIDER

## 4 THE CHRISTMAS RAID

General Bragg did have a strategic concern - to reverse the Union advance through Tennessee, reoccupy that Southern state, and turn Kentucky to the Confederacy. To accomplish this task Bragg had to first stop the flow of war materials for Rosencrans' army into Nashville.

He assigned General John Hunt Morgan to break Rosecrans' Louisville and Nashville Railroad supply line somewhere in Kentucky. The L&N Railroad carried food, forage, and supplies from Louisville through the uneven terrain of Kentucky to the Union army's depot at Nashville. Reports were that the L&N tracks were heavily guarded to prepare for the push on Bragg.

The ever-confident Morgan believed that, regardless of the fortifications, a weakness could be found just north of Elizabethtown in an area known generally as Muldraugh Hill.

Muldraugh Hill is an escarpment rising from the Ohio River to an elevation of over 400 feet in just five miles and crisscrossed by streams and gorges.

*Editors' Note: Our family is very familiar with this hill which is located in northern Hardin County, north of Elizabethtown. We have travelled it many times in automobile, and it is an imposing hill to climb. Breaking the railroad line at this point would cause months of delay while repairs were made.*

Morgan's knowledge of the area probably came from the experience of his brother-in-law and second in command, Colonel Basil Duke who in 1861 had walked through the area avoiding Federal capture in Elizabethtown. In early fall of 1861 Duke was in Elizabethtown and had just recruited two companies of Confederates. He was preparing to swear them in on the courthouse square when they were taken by surprise by the lead elements of General William Sherman's force that had come to Elizabethtown from Fort Duffield near West Point, Kentucky - just a few miles north of Muldraugh Hill.

*Editors' Note: During the Civil War it was not unknown for commanders to have relatives and friends having important posts within their commands. This practice was especially true because many units were organized from towns or counties within states. Morgan was no exception to this practice. Friends and relations served under Morgan.*

The unfortunate timing of Federal force's arrival resulted in the both companies of Confederate recruits scattering in all directions. Colonel Duke and another officer made their escape by walking southward on the L&N railroad tracks from Elizabethtown in the hope of catching a train that would eventually take them to Lexington.

Instead of meeting a train, a handcar of Federal soldiers traveling south rolled into view. In spite of Duke's efforts to conceal his identity, a couple of the passengers recognized him and the other man as a Confederate officers. Colonel Duke now found himself in serious trouble because he was behind enemy lines dressed as a civilian. He could have been hanged as spy.

Just as Duke was about to be apprehended, he had a change of fortune. One of the Federals riding the handcar was his old friend and Transylvania schoolmate, John Harlan, who realized Duke's predicament. As one of the Federals attempted to apply the brakes, Harlan placed his foot between the deck and the brake handle keeping it from being fully engaged. Duke made his getaway through a cornfield as the handcar continued forward and disappeared into a tunnel.

When it was obvious that no Federal pursuit was being made, Duke continued his trip through Muldraugh Hill. He certainly would have noticed the two huge wooden trestles that elevated the tracks above deep gorges - both about ninety feet high and 500 feet long. These trestles - located in very difficult terrain - became the primary targets of the Christmas Raid.

December 22, 1862, dawned bright and sunny in Alexandria, Tennessee, where Morgan organized his force and prepared to depart. Bragg had approved the raid into Kentucky as more or less a last resort to try to disrupt Rosecrans' plans for a winter campaign. In fact before Morgan left, one of Bragg's corps commanders, General William Hardee, had told Morgan that it would be impossible to burn the bridges.

Regardless of the doubts and obvious risks, Morgan kissed his twenty-one year-old bride of eight days goodbye and, after pausing to watch her carriage disappear around a curve in the road, he passed orders to Colonel Duke to begin the march.

Morgan moved the largest Confederate force he had ever commanded - approximately 4,000 strong, toward Tompkinsville. He reached that town by nightfall of December 23rd.

As they camped that night, the men were glad to be on their native soil of Kentucky once again. Approximately ninety percent of Morgan's brigade were Kentuckians who had not been home since they had enlisted.

One of Morgan's officers, Lieutenant McCreary put his emotions into words as he confided to his diary:

> *Tonight we are camped on the sacred soil of Kentucky, and it fills my heart with joy and pride.*

The next day was Christmas Eve. Morgan continued to Glasgow, Kentucky, under gray clouds and a cold wind that cut through the men. They arrived at Glasgow about mid-afternoon and routed the Federal garrison stationed there.

They continued across the Green River on Christmas, brushing aside any Federal forces in their path. On Christmas evening they camped in a cold rain just outside of Upton, Kentucky, where a Union garrison guarded the railroad track.

The next morning in a move to keep the Union commanders from guessing his true objective, Morgan sent a detachment south toward the site of a previous victory - the Bacon Creek railroad bridge near Bonnieville, Kentucky. About one hundred Union soldiers were fortified in a blockhouse near the bridge. This garrison gave Morgan's detachment a brief but ferocious fight that resulted in the destruction of the bridge for the third time during the war. Morgan's men destroyed the track and burned crossties on their way back to their camp in Upton.

During this raid, protracted resistance was rare. Most of the garrisons that were challenged quickly surrendered after Colonel Duke made a show of the artillery.

In Upton, George "Lightning" Ellsworth cut the telegraph lines and then sent confusing information about Morgan's location, his troop strength, and intentions to all of the Federal officers in the area. Ellsworth was a Canadian who had met Morgan in Lexington, Kentucky. Ellsworth received his

The Christmas Raid

nickname during Morgan's first raid when he sat on a railroad crosstie knee-deep in water during a thunderstorm near Horse Cave, Kentucky.

Morgan quickly realized the importance of the telegraph not only for communicating with his superiors, but in spreading confusion amongst the enemy. Ellsworth was particularly helpful in this endeavor - he was adept at quickly reading Morse code and also of imitating the styles of other telegraphers.

The morning of December 27th dawned cold, but the sky was clearing. Morgan and his regiment rode toward Elizabethtown. Upon arriving, Morgan threw a cordon around the town and set his artillery on a hill commanding the entire area.

The Federals had set up a strong defensive positions near the railroad by fortifying a number of brick warehouses complete with loopholes though which the soldiers could fire their muskets. Stockades were under construction but not completed when Morgan arrived.

About 650 soldiers of the 91st Illinois Volunteer Infantry Regiment commanded by Colonel H.S. Smith were garrisoned in the town. Colonel Smith knew the hopelessness of his situation but was determined to give Morgan his best effort by first attempting to fool the Confederate commander into believing that a larger Federal force occupied the town. Smith did this by marching his men in double file loop across the brow of a hill in full view to give Morgan the impression that he commanded much greater numbers. Next Smith sent Morgan word that a Federal force had Morgan surrounded and he should surrender immediately.

Neither ruse worked. After repeated requests that Smith surrender, Morgan gave the citizens of Elizabethtown thirty minutes to evacuate the women and children.

Colonel Smith and the 91st Illinois were at a tactical disadvantage. His men were scattered among the various warehouses buildings. Smith could not coordinate his units.

General Morgan used his six-to-one advantage of men and seven pieces of artillery to perfection. The Union soldiers were overpowered in short time.

With the Confederate artillery covering their movements, Morgan sent two brigades forward into the streets. As the Confederates moved into town the artillery shells screamed over their heads.

Before the Confederates could close with the enemy, they had to ford the rain-swollen Valley Creek. The Southerners waded through the freezing, waist-deep water, holding their muskets above their heads while the artillery kept most of the Federals under cover. All Colonel Smith could do was to attempt to delay the inevitable.

As the battle continued, many of the town's people recognized that the buildings around the public square housing the 91st Illinois were receiving the most of the punishment. Many citizens sought shelter at the home of Samuel Beal Thomas. Mr. Thomas was the county's first millionaire and a personal friend of General Morgan. Many in town knew of their relationship and went there in hopes that General Morgan would not level his guns at his old friend. This place sheltered a few civilians briefly but then came under fire when Morgan saw a number of Union soldiers following the civilians to the home of his old friend.

With the missiles doing their deadly work, the advancing Confederate brigades engaged isolated Federal soldiers in house-to-house fighting, soon handkerchiefs, bed cloths, and anything white began emerging from windows and doorways all over town. Before surrendering, however, Colonel Smith was wounded in the face when a shell struck the house from which he was fighting.

Smith was enraged with his men who had participated in the various unauthorized surrender of the town, since he had not ordered it. As Duke recalled years later,

> *Smith was not ready to surrender, but his men were not going to wait on him and ran out of the houses and threw down their arms.*

Confederate sympathies in Elizabethtown were strong, and the residents were glad to throw off the Federal occupation, if only for a little while. The Confederate invaders were treated like conquering heroes and provided with whiskey, Christmas goodies, and entertainment (www.HardinKyHistory.org).

On the next day - December 28th - Morgan moved to his primary objective - the railroad trestles at Muldraugh Hill. Sweeping aside the Union garrison, Morgan's troops burned the trestles to the ground. A significant break in Rosecrans' supply line was made.

On December 29th Federals finally caught Morgan's expeditionary force at the Rolling Fork River near Boston, Kentucky. Morgan's command of about 4,000

Confederates was surprised by Colonel John Marshall Harlan's 3,000 Union troops. Morgan and his senior officers had just finished a meeting in the Hamilton-Hall House when Harlan opened with artillery fire from the high ground to the south of Morgan's resting troops.

Colonel Duke was commanding Morgan's rear guard of three hundred men. Duke was reinforced by a detachment of eight hundred men commanded by Colonel Roy Cluke. Cluke's detachment had returned after abandoning plans to burn the L&N trestle over the Rolling Fork near Lebanon Junction. Duke was charged with defending the two main fords on the river, the first one-quarter mile south and the second one-third mile west.

Harlan commanded a mixture of infantry and cavalry, plus six parrot rifles (small cannon). The parrots opened a barrage on Duke's small command as he was trying to hold the Federals in check long enough for the Confederates to ford the stream. In the attack Duke was struck in the head with a shell fragment and he fell from his horse. Captain Tom Quirk carried the unconscious Duke to Bardstown on horseback, where he received medical aid. Duke's stand allowed Morgan's men enough time to get to the second, western, ford and escape Harlan's trap. Before the war Harlan and Duke were friends. Both graduates of Centre College and Transylvania Law School.

Morgan by now, with his primary objective attained, determined to continue southward to rejoin Bragg's army. In the early morning hours of December 30th, three companies of Morgan's 9th Kentucky Cavalry, supported by a single 12-pound mountain howitzer, arrived at New Haven, Kentucky, and demanded the surrender of the Federal garrison. The garrison, commanded by Captain John K. Allen, consisted of Company H, 78th Illinois Infantry Regiment - about ninety strong. The Federals occupied a small stockade at the west end of the L&N Railroad bridge at New Haven. The Union garrison was outnumbered more than two-to-one by the 220 Confederates.

Colonel William H. Benneson, commander of the 78th Illinois Infantry Regiment was in New Haven when the Confederates attacked. Benneson assumed command of the garrison and respectfully declined the Confederate demand for surrender.

The fighting began with Confederate artillery fire from 1,000 yards northeast of the stockade. The Confederates shelled the Union troops for over an hour moving their gun several times to get closer to the Union defenders. When the Confederates had closed to within 800 yards, the Union soldiers opened fire.

The Union fire drew in the Confederate cavalrymen; they dismounted, deployed, and returned fire. After thirty minutes, the heavy fire from the Federal infantry drove off the main Confederate attack.

The Confederates tried once more. They attempted to flank the stockade from north of the railroad embankment. Union fire again drove the Confederates back. The Southern troops withdrew taking their dead and wounded with them. The Union soldiers suffered no casualties, but the artillery fire damaged several buildings in New Haven, including both taverns. Confederate losses were reported as two killed and ten wounded.

As a portion of his force successfully engaged the enemy at New Haven, the remainder made every effort to reach the Cumberland River at Burkesville before the Union forces did and cut off Morgan's retreat. The weather had turned bad - even for December in Kentucky. Cold, drizzling rain turned into sleet and the roads began to freeze.

On the evening of December 30, 1862, 3,900 Morgan's force overwhelmed the little Kentucky town of Springfield in Washington County. On arriving at Springfield, the weary Confederates were directed to encamp on the Lebanon Road where they slept the best they could. The soldiers lit fires in the streets and fields. The men slept on anything they could find.

A few men found more pleasant accommodations. Lieutenant George B. Eastin was among the men enjoying a hot meal at the home of Confederate sympathizer C.T. Cunningham.

Union troops were closing the trap on Morgan's forces in Springfield. Under the cover of near blizzard conditions and total darkness, a Union cavalry patrol advanced down East Main Street of Springfield, opened fire on Confederate artillery, and then hastily withdrew.

Realizing the danger of his situation, Morgan decided on a night march in the blizzard. He "drafted" two local citizens to guide him down the Elizabethtown Pike to the Campbellsville-Lebanon Road. Morgan's selected route passed around the Union forces at Lebanon on an old dirt road. Before midnight Morgan's whole column was moving.

Morgan's men occupied Campbellsville on New Year's Eve. They entered a warehouse and seized the supplies, foodstuffs, funds, mail, and other valuables.

Curtis Burke, a scout riding with Morgan, wrote about Campbellsville:

> *No Yanks there except a few sick in the hospital. Our company camped in a stable ... I went to a house and got my supper. I was running around most of the night hunting for things the Yanks hid away. A crowd of us got into a room where there were four large boxes full of new cavalry overcoats, pants and boots.*

The next morning the townspeople heard that Morgan had ordered his men to set fire to the remaining stores that they could not carry. The citizens protested vehemently, fearing that a fire would spread and burn down the entire town. They persuaded the Confederate commanding officer to remove the remaining stores from the building and place them in the middle of Main Street before setting fire to them.

The Confederates continued southward through Tebbs Bend, Kentucky, where a stockade and bridge were burned. Morgan reached Tennessee and Bragg's army in early January of 1863 (www.TrailsRUs.com).

Morgan was returning as Bragg was in retrograde from Murfreesboro to Tullahoma. Morgan's wife, Martha moved with Army of Tennessee. During the retreat she wrote to her new husband:

> *I had some dark days, dearest, and when the battle was raging around me in such fury, and everybody from the Commander-in-Chief to the privates were praying for "Morgan to come." ...There was one continual inquiry at the front door - "When will Morgan be here?"*

Bragg certainly wanted to know where Morgan was. He had sent orders to Morgan that were never received.

Once again, General John Hunt Morgan had provided the South with an inspiring and romantic lightning attack deep into territory controlled by the Union. As exciting as the raid was, one must ask honestly if it accomplished anything for the South.

The Christmas Raid did cause strategic damage to the North. Railroad and telegraph lines were cut and bridges were destroyed. These successes did slow the Union advance by denying and disrupting supplies and communications to them. In addition Morgan's raids (and those of others) provided the Confederate government with propaganda victories to inspire their populace and to strike fear into the people of the North. With the exception of General Robert E. Lee's march to Gettysburg, Pennsylvania, cavalry raids were the only means by which the Confederates could take the battle to the population of the North.

It must be said, however, that though these raids were strategically significant, they had very little impact on the immediate tactical situation. In the Second Battle of Murfreesboro, for example, Morgan and Forrest were so far removed from battlefield, that Rosecrans gave them no consideration as he was making tactical decisions. On the other side, Bragg hampered himself by sending two-thirds of his cavalry so far from Murfreesboro. What, then, were the reasons for Morgan's Great Raid?

## 5 REASONS FOR THE GREAT RAID

The year 1863 began with a winter lull in the fighting. The Union continued its execution of the War Departments "Anaconda Plan" - developed by General-in-Chief Winfield Scott. The plan was to surround the

primary Confederate states with a blockade along the Atlantic Ocean and the Gulf of Mexico, and seizure of the Mississippi River and Ohio River. With the "Old South" surrounded the Union would then both squeeze and then slice into southern territory from all sides.

On the Mississippi, Grant moved southward to place Vicksburg under siege, and Banks moved northward to lay siege to Port Hudson. Vicksburg and Port Hudson fell in early July 1863.

In the east the Union was defeated at the battle of Chancellorsville in May. In June General Robert E. Lee crossed the Potomac River and began his northward march that would end in the Battle of Gettysburg.

In June General Rosecrans began moving his Union Army of the Cumberland against General Bragg's Army of Tennessee. It is this movement that forms the background for General Morgan's Great Raid.

In June Rosecrans' line was centered on Murfreesboro. Bragg's line was located about twenty-five miles south of Rosecrans and north of Tullahoma, Tennessee - Bragg's headquarters. Morgan's brigade was deployed on the Confederate right flank in McMinnville, Tennessee.

On June 23rd Bragg was maneuvered out of his positions, and Rosecrans moved to within twelve mile of Tullahoma. Both armies took up defensive positions and awaited a battle.

Once more Rosecrans feinted and drew the Confederates off their positions. Clearly outflanked, Bragg realized that he had to retreat to Chattanooga. He called on Morgan to create a diversion in Rosecrans' rear area - in Kentucky.

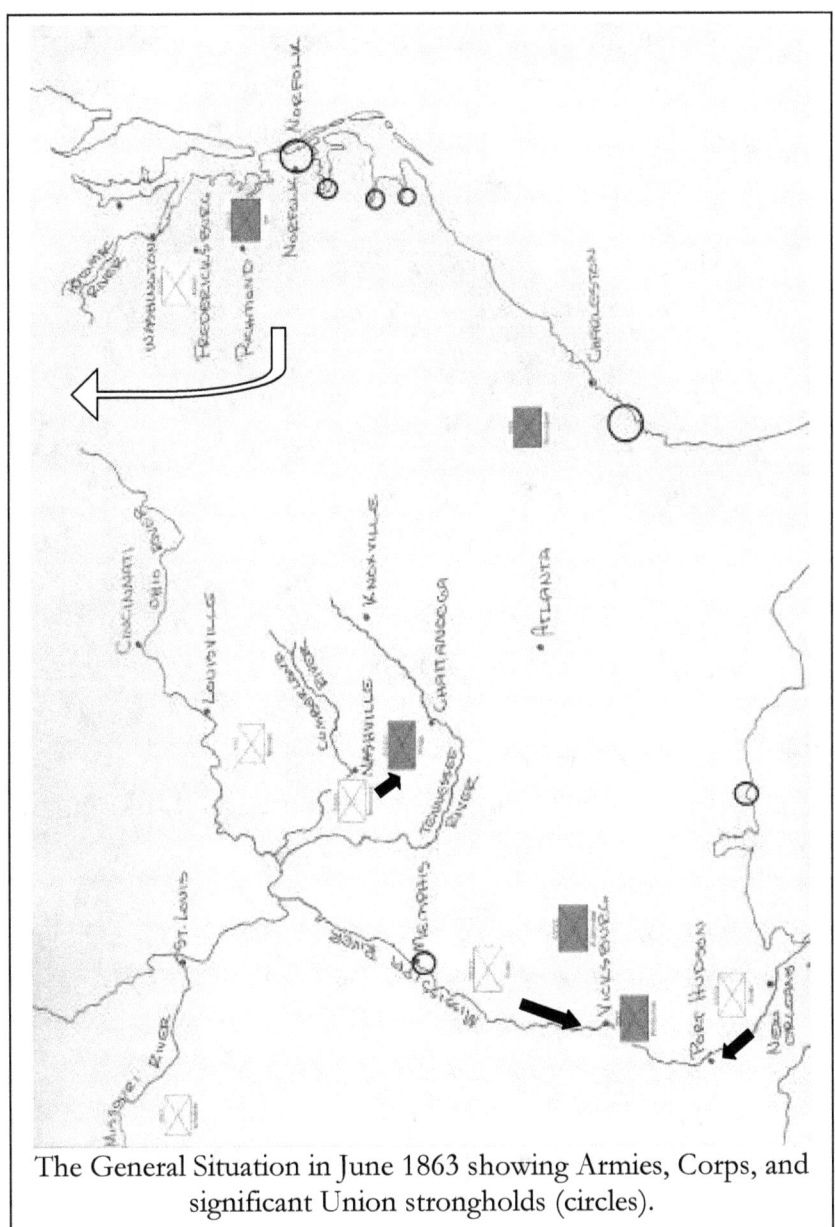

The General Situation in June 1863 showing Armies, Corps, and significant Union strongholds (circles).

Morgan looked forward to this order to go northward once again. It is evident that Morgan hoped to be of assistance to General Robert E. Lee who was advancing into Pennsylvania. Although Morgan's desires may appear to be a far-fetched dream, still there is indication that supporting Lee was what Morgan had hoped to do. Duke, his chief-of-staff, wrote in his memoirs:

> *[Morgan] had ordered me three weeks previously to send intelligent men to examine the fords of the upper Ohio - that at Buffington among them - and it is a fact of which others, as well as myself are cognizant, that he intended - long before he crossed the Ohio - to make no effort to re-cross it, except at some of these fords, unless he found it more expedient, when he reached that region, to join General Lee, if the latter should still be in Pennsylvania.* (Duke, p411)

Bragg anticipated this desire on the part of his independently-minded cavalry commander. Duke again recorded Bragg's specific orders:

> *General Bragg refused [Morgan] permission to make the raid as he desired to make it and ordered him to confine himself to Kentucky. I was not present at the interview between them, but General Morgan told me that he intended, notwithstanding his orders, to cross the Ohio.* (Duke, p410.)

After the war Bragg disclaimed all responsibility for Morgan's drive into Ohio, and no orders can be found that authorized Morgan to do so. General Joseph Wheeler, who commanded another cavalry brigade under Bragg, states:

> ...*[Morgan] was urged by me to observe the importance of his returning to our army as rapidly as possible. I make this point apparent, as it is the one to which my attention was particularly called.*
> (Official Records, series 1, volume 23.)

So, one motivation for the Great Raid was Morgan's own desire to march northward - and particularly to join Lee in Pennsylvania. One can only conjecture that Morgan may have wanted to escape Bragg's leadership for that of Lee's, or to join with an army that was advancing instead of retreating. Possibly, Morgan saw that a successful deep plunge northward - that Lee was executing - was the only hope for victory by the South.

Still another motivation for the Great Raid is best described by a note appended to the diary of J.B. Jones who was a clerk in the Confederate War Department at Richmond, Virginia. Jones writes in his diary on July 18, 1863, "General Morgan is in the enemy's country." The notation made later says, "The fatal Ohio raid, launched probably at Clement Laird Vallandigham's request [was intended] to rally the Copperheads in Indiana, Ohio, and join Lee in Pennsylvania." (Jones, p382)

This motivation somewhat conflicts with Bragg's own instructions to Morgan, but it is certainly plausible that an Ohio raid would have been seen as supportive of an uprising of the Copperheads in the North.

Vallandigham was an Ohio politician, and leader of the anti-war Democrats - called Copperheads - during the American Civil War. He served two terms in the

United States House of Representatives from 1858 to 1863.

Support for this possible motive is found in the writings of John W. Headley, a lieutenant in Morgan's brigade who was detached from this duty and assigned to the Confederate Secret Service for work in the United States and Canada. Headley writes:

> *Mr. Vallandigham returned to Ohio about the middle of June [1863]. He made speeches immediately... In his first speech he almost declared the existence and purposes of the [Sons of Liberty]. He said: "But I warn also those men in power that there is a vast multitude, a host whom they cannot number, bound together by the holiest ties, to defend ... their natural and constitutional rights as free men at all hazards and to the last extremity. ...The 20$^{th}$ of July seemed to have been determined upon as the date of out-spoken declaration of resistance.* (Headley, pp223, 232)

There are other indications of a coordination of resistance to the war in the North. On June 11, 1863, the deputy provost marshal for Rush County, Indiana, was assassinated and his assistant wounded by two men concealed in a wheat field. Another military draft officer was murdered in Sullivan County on June 18$^{th}$. In this latter instance the crime was attributed to an organized group - presumably members of the Knights of the Golden Circle.

The KGC was a secret society that was seeking to annex Mexico, central American, and the Caribbean for inclusion in the United States as slave states. Members of the KGC had been holding military drills in the area for sometime. In reporting on the affair and official estimated that in this and the adjoining congressional districts there were at least 1,200 men secretly under arms. (Gray and Wood, p137)

In June of 1862 Governor Oliver Morton of Indiana wrote to Edwin Stanton, Secretary of War under Lincoln. The governor reported the existence of a secret political organization in Indiana of an estimated strength of 10,000 members whose ascertainable purposes included the obstruction of recruiting, opposition to the collecting of taxes for war purposes and, in general, the fostering of distrust of the constituted authorities. (Gray, p92)

There is evidence of fear by Federal officials of a collaboration between the KGC and Morgan (Official Records, series 3, volume 3):

> *Office of Acting Assistant Provost Marshal*
> *Indianapolis, July 10, 1863*
> *Sir: In consequence of Morgan's Raid into this State and the fears I entertain that there is an understanding between him and the Knights of the Golden Circle, I have instructed the several Provost Marshals that in the event of the militia being called away ... the roll is to be so secreted as to put it out of the power of the domestic enemies to find them. The militia of the State is being called out and ... domestic traitors may embrace this opportunity to destroy the roll.*
> *Colonel and Actg. Asst. Prov. Marshal*

*General for Indiana*

Morgan had a good idea of this attitude of resistance to the war and the support of the South in the northern states - especially along the border. Captain Thomas Hines of Morgan's command had been on a reconnoitering expedition for Morgan some few weeks before the raid, and Morgan had sent spies into the North to chart a path for the raid if the opportunity developed.

Jones of the Confederate War Department recalled in his diary in February 1863:

> *A letter from Lieutenant Colonel R.A. Alston, Decatur, Georgia, says Captain _____, one of General Morgan's secret agents, has just arrived there after spending several months in the North, and reports that Lincoln cannot recruit his armies by draft, or any other mode, unless they achieve some signal success in the spring campaign. He says, moreover, that there is a perfect organization, all over the North, for the purpose of revolution and the expulsion of death of the Abolitionists and free negroes; and this organization Generals _____ and _____ are the military leaders. Colonel A. asked permission of the Secretary of War to go into southern Illinois, where, he is confident, if he contributes to precipitate civil war, he can, at least, bring out thousands of men who will fight for the Southern cause.* (Jones, p155)

It seems clear that the raid into Ohio was based upon a real hope of fomenting revolt and adding great numbers to the Confederate banner. Morgan must have listened to the reports of well-meaning but over-enthusiastic spies. It was to gain recruits for the cause that he continually ventured into Kentucky in the early period of the war and it is not too far amiss to assume that the raid became a raid into the North, and not simply a diversion in Kentucky, for this same reason. One need not assume that there was an order from the Confederate War Department to Morgan that excluded Bragg. Morgan simply took the matter into his hands.

It is clear that circumstances presented Morgan with an opportunity to take the Union at a low ebb. Who could say but what a well-timed raid into the North would bring great support to the South? There was reason to expect it - or at least to be hopeful. The fate of the Union at the end of June, 1863, seemed to hang upon the military fortunes of the next month.

On July 8th General John Hunt Morgan crossed into Indiana. It was not an aimless act of bravado. It was a intentional - and hopeful - move by a general who was aware of the precarious strategic situation.

# WILLIAM WOODROW SLIDER

# 6 THROUGH KENTUCKY

On July 2, 1863, the expeditionary force under Brigadier John Hunt Morgan entered the Commonwealth of Kentucky in high spirits. The regiments had been infiltrating into Cumberland County, Kentucky, from Sparta, Tennessee, since late June.

Morgan's force numbered approximately 2,500 effective cavalrymen divided into two provisional brigades. The first brigade, commanded by Colonel Basil Duke, had 1,500 men and two three-inch parrot guns as artillery. The second brigade, commanded by Colonel Adam Johnson, had 1,000 riders and two twelve-pound howitzers.

*Editors' note: Some estimates number Morgan's force at 4,000 riders. The reason for the larger number may be the inclusion of supporting troops.*

The First Brigade crossed the Cumberland River at Burkesville, Scott's Ferry, Amandaville and Bakerton. The crossing took the better part of two days. The Second Brigade crossed the Cumberland at McMillan's Ferry, Salt Lick Bend and other points to the west. So many fords were used that the initial reports had Morgan's force numbered at 10,000.

The Federal commander along the Kentucky-Tennessee border, General Henry Moses Judah, assumed that the high water of the Cumberland River would be a barrier to any

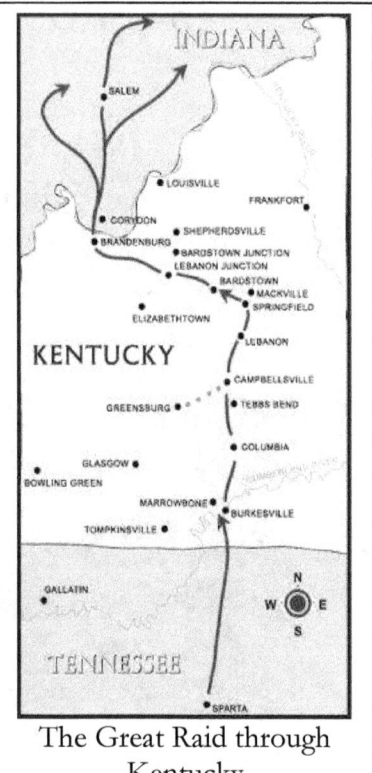

The Great Raid through Kentucky

Confederate raiders. Due to heavy rains in late June, the river was out of its banks - over a half mile wide in some places. Consequently, Gen. Edward H. Hobson, defending at Marrowbone just ten miles away, had few troops at hand.

At the Burkesville crossing, Colonel Duke sent the brigade across in groups of one hundred. The troops placed their saddles and blankets on an old flatboat. Their horses, forced to swim across the river, were claimed on the other side. Legend has it that Duke's men crossed naked except for their individual weapons and ammunition, formed for battle, and then swept aside the light opposition.

Shortly after that engagement, General James M. Shackelford's brigade arrived to support General Edward Hobson. Immediately, several cavalry and infantry regiments were dispatched, under Shackelford's command, in pursuit of Morgan. For some unknown reason, however, Hobson's superior officer, General Judah, ordered Shackelford's force to return to Marrowbone.

Later on the same day (July 2nd), Morgan occupied the square around the Cumberland County Courthouse at Burkesville and waited for provisions. At the river, wagons had to be unloaded, disassembled, and loaded on makeshift rafts; then reassembled and the cargo reloaded on the other side. The men soon tired of waiting for the rations, and rode northward, foraging for food at farmhouses on the way.

After the first wave of Morgan's 1st Brigade crossed the Cumberland, the general sent scouts under Captain Tom Quirk to reconnoiter west of Burkesville and to draw the attention of the Union garrison at Marrowbone, commanded by General Hobson, away from the 2nd Brigade that was crossing the Cumberland.

The Confederate scouts galloped out of Burkesville on the Glasgow Road toward the 3,000 Union soldiers at Marrowbone. The scouts brushed aside the Union pickets and were joined by Colonel W.W. Ward's 9th Tennessee Cavalry Regiment and Colonel J. W. Grigsby's 6th Kentucky Cavalry Regiment. This unit, commanded by Morgan himself, ambushed a Union cavalry column of three hundred riders. The Federals reversed direction and retreated swiftly. The Southerners pursued.

The cloud of dust that the retreating Union cavalry raised obscured the vision of the pursuing Confederates. They could not see a regiment of Northern infantry which had formed for battle.

One of Captain Quirk's scouts spotted the deployed infantry. He grabbed the reins of Morgan's mount and stopped the pursuit, thereby avoiding a Confederate disaster.

The Southern cavalry sent a volley into Union infantry at short range. The Confederates sustained the loss of two dead and two wounded. Federal losses were five killed and fifteen wounded.

Captain Quirk himself received a wound to his left wrist that was so severe that his rein arm was broken and he had to return to Tennessee. This small battle took Morgan's chief scout out of action for the Great Raid. This loss would have an serious impact on the future of the Great Raid.

Morgan continued northward. At Columbia Colonel Frank Lane Wolford threw his "Wild Riders" - the 1st

Kentucky Cavalry Regiment (USA) numbering about 150 soldiers in the path of Morgan's force. They were joined by elements of the 2nd and 45th Ohio Infantry regiments.

Wolford, an Adair County native, organized his "Wild Riders" 1861. His men knew little about the drill and discipline, but had great confidence in their leader.

Captain J.C. Cassel of Morgan's advance guard was wounded. Captain Cassel was placed in an ambulance where he remained for the entire raid.

Following the Columbia engagement on the afternoon of July 3rd, Morgan's force continued northward on the Columbia-Lebanon Pike. Just beyond Columbia, they passed a small union camp that was powerless to stop the raiders. On that evening the Confederates camped in the fields around Cane Valley.

Many of the raiders had abandoned their horses in Columbia - exchanging fresh mounts without consent of their owners. They took whatever supplies they could - including whiskey and money - because there was no supply train with them. Farmers and shopkeepers had their storehouses emptied. Lieutenant Colonel Robert Alston, of Morgan's staff, considered such behavior appalling and remarked that some men accompanied the army simply for plunder.

On July 4th the raiders arrived at Tebbs Bend on the Green River where they encountered the 25th Michigan Infantry Regiment. The regiment of about 1,000 men, organized into eleven companies, was commanded by Colonel Orlando H. Moore. The regiment was deployed within a stockade that was perfectly situated and rendered a direct assault necessary to carry it. Morgan was thus disposed to parley and, therefore, called upon

Colonel Moore to surrender. Moore refused, saying in retrospect that "the Fourth of July was no day for me to entertain such a proposition." (Young, p372)

Colonel Johnson assaulted the works with two regiments which were stopped and hurled back. The 11th Kentucky Regiment rushed to the rescue, were slowed, stopped, and pushed back. Thirty-six Confederates were killed, and forty-five wounded. Among the casualties were some of the outstanding officers. The Confederates withdrew and left the defenders unmolested.

Morgan by-passed the stockade and the raid continued through Campbellsville. In Campbellsville local resident Joseph H. Chandler, an attorney, a strong Union Democrat, and a Kentucky State Representative was scheduled to speak on the Courthouse lawn at a Fourth of July ceremony with U.S. Congressman Aaron Harding. The 1:00pm ceremony was cancelled when Morgan's troops entered Campbellsville from the south following their loss at Tebbs Bend. The Rebels fanned out to farms within five miles of the town to find forage for their horses and food for themselves.

The raiders proceeded without incident to the outskirts of Lebanon. At the approaches to Lebanon a civilian was taken prisoner, and while in custody his watch was stolen by Captain Murphy. Murphy was reported by Captain Magenis and was arrested. While under arrest, Murphy approached Magenis and shot him dead.

On the morning of July 5th the Confederate troops attacked Lebanon. The town was garrisoned by the 20th Kentucky Regiment (USA) and two Michigan regiments commanded by Lieutenant Colonel Charles S. Hanson, whose brother, Roger, was a Confederate general.

Hanson knew Morgan was coming and he made what preparations he could. Hanson deployed most of his 350 men behind a barricade of fences, overturned wagons, and other obstructions. He realized that this skirmish line could only slow the Confederate advance on the city. He planned to make his stand at the L&N railroad depot and other brick buildings once his skirmish line was pushed back.

Upon reaching Lebanon, Morgan demanded Hanson's surrender. Hanson refused and Morgan attacked with artillery and dismounted cavalry. Morgan's nearly ten-to-one advantage quickly overwhelmed the Union soldiers, pushing them into town where most sought refuge in the depot.

The brick depot, a block off Main Street, provided a strong defensive position. Its location was such that Morgan could not use his artillery effectively against it. When Hanson refused a second demand for surrender, Morgan ordered nearby buildings set on fire. Finally, after nearly seven hours of fighting, with the roof of the depot and much of the town on fire, the 2nd Kentucky (CSA) cleared the depot, and Hanson surrendered.

This battle was costly for Morgan. Hanson's small garrison held him up for seven hours, inflicting some fifty casualties

During the Battle of Lebanon, Lieutenant Tom Morgan, the nineteen year-old brother of General Morgan, was killed near "Sunnyside," the home of Presbyterian minister T.H. Cleland. During the fighting

General Morgan time and again ordered the youngest Morgan to the rear to keep him out of harm's way, but Tom refused to sit out the battle. According to legend Tom Morgan was shot and killed leading a group of men in the final charge against the depot.

The death of Tom Morgan enraged Morgan and his men. The Confederate soldiers looted stores and burned about twenty buildings. The Union prisoners were then marched some ten miles at the double-quick to Springfield where they were paroled. Several Union prisoners died on the forced march. Miraculously, Union losses were small. Hanson reported four killed and sixteen wounded.

When Colonel Hanson surrendered the depot, Charlton Morgan, another brother, is said to have grabbed Hanson by the beard and say, "I'll blow your brains out you ... rascal." Fellow soldiers restrained Charlton before he could carry out his threat.

Afterwards, General Morgan is said to have told Colonel Hanson, "Charlie, the next time you see [my] mother you be damn ... sure to tell her you killed brother Tom." Hanson and Morgan were the best of friends before the war.

That night Tom Morgan was laid out in the parlor of "Sunnyside." On the next day, he was buried in a rose garden on the west side of the house. His body remained there until 1867, when the Morgan family retrieved the body and buried it in the family plot in the Lexington Cemetery.

The expedition immediately moved toward Springfield where Company "H" of the 2nd Kentucky was detached to Harrodsburg in order to draw away the Union cavalry.

On the morning of July 5, 1863, Springfield awoke to the roar of cannon fire coming from Lebanon. That afternoon John Hunt Morgan's column reached Springfield with over three hundred Federal prisoners-of-war. Colonel Duke and Major William J. Davis from South Carolina entered the town with the lead elements and paroled the prisoners at the courthouse.

Upon leaving Springfield, Morgan instructed Davis' forces to create a diversion, hoping to cover his crossing of the Ohio River at Brandenburg. While attempting to do so, Davis and his men encountered Union troops and Davis was captured.

Captain Ralph Sheldon leading Company "C" of the 2nd Kentucky Cavalry descended on Bardstown on Sunday morning July 5, 1863. They drove the hand full of Union troops occupying Bardstown into a livery stable two blocks north of the courthouse. Lieutenant Thomas W. Sullivan of the 4th U. S. Cavalry took up position in the livery stable and defended it for several hours against the attacking Confederates.

After the initial assault, Sheldon demanded the Union troops surrender. Sullivan rejected the demand, and the battle resumed and continued into the evening. To prevent the trapped Union soldiers from escaping Capt. Sheldon had his men stretch ropes across the street. The Confederates attempted to set the stable on fire, but the Union soldiers doused the fire and continued their defense.

Just before daylight on Monday morning, July 6th, Gen. John Hunt Morgan arrived from Springfield with the main force. Sheldon was sent again to demand the surrender. It is reported that Sheldon informed Sullivan, "If you refuse, we will blow you to ... with our artillery."

Sullivan replied, "I am obliged to the General's kind intentions, but it is our duty to trouble him a little longer." When Sheldon returned from the parley, small arms fire resumed. Soon the Confederates were massed for an assault and four artillery pieces were positioned to fire on the livery stable.

Sullivan realized his situation was hopeless. Carrying a flag of truce he immerged from the building, but Richard Morgan immediately refused his surrender, "Go back," he said, "you have already refused these terms twice. You have no right to demand them now."

With no other options Sullivan returned to the stable and prepared for the Confederate attack. General Morgan then sent a messenger with a flag of truce and demanded the unconditional surrender of the Federals. They agreed.

General Morgan, it has been said, yelled at the Union soldiers as they left the stable, "You twenty-five ... Yankees have cost me twenty-four hours."

Shortly after the surrender, at about 10:00am on July 6th Morgan's command left Bardstown on the Shepherdsville Road on the way to the Ohio River.

At Bardstown Morgan detached two companies under the command of Captain Davis. This small force was to seize riverboats at Twelve Mile Island and to occupy militia in that vicinity. They were to rejoin Morgan and the main force at Salem, Indiana.

*Editors' Note: Twelve Mile Island is located north (upstream) of Louisville on the Ohio River. The island is bisected by the border between Jefferson and Oldham counties in Kentucky. When we were younger the two of us would sail near Twelve Mile Island and observe the tangle of trees and undergrowth from the river.*

Morgan also sent an advance party to his primary river crossing - Brandenburg. Captains H. Clay Merriwether and Samuel Taylor and their men encamped on farms in and around Brandenburg.

*Author's Note: Boling states that Morgan went from Lebannon to Elizabethtown and was there fired upon by sharpshooters. According to this lone source Morgan captured about fifteen of the sharpshooters, marched them a few miles west of town, and had them shot. No other source records Morgan passing near Elizabethtown on the Great Raid.*

At Brandenburg Merriweather and Taylor were joined by Captain Thomas Hines, who had been sent to Clinton County as commandant of a rest camp for the 9th Kentucky Regiment. Hines had gained permission to raid north of the Cumberland River and had taken the initiative to stretch his raid into Indiana. With about forty men he spent over two weeks raiding as far north as Seymour where he was met by Indiana militia and turned back. Hines and much of his small unit evaded capture and swam across the river on the same day as Morgan's lead element arrived at Brandenburg.

This lead element of the Confederates placed one cannon on East Hill in Brandenburg and a second on

West Hill. Shortly after noon on July 7, 1863 the mailboat, *John T. McCombs*, arrived and docked at the foot of Main Street. The Confederates stormed the boat and captured it without firing a shot.

They then moved the *McCombs* to mid-stream where they hoisted distress flags. The *Alice Dean*, a luxury boat carrying passengers to Louisville came in sight. The side-wheel packet owned by the Dean Company of Cincinnati, Ohio, shifted course and came alongside the *Combs* to offer assistance. The Confederates boarded the *Dean* and captured it - also without firing a shot.

The boats were tied together and steamed to the Brandenburg dock. All passengers were put ashore with a warning not to raise an alarm. The Confederates treated the passengers of both boats with the utmost respect; even returning $10,000 the passengers of the *Dean* had placed in the safe in the purser's office. (www.TrailsRUs.com)

*Editors' Note: Our family is very familiar with the Brandenburg area. Dad served Brandenburg Methodist Church twice as pastor — the second time when he was married to Mom. Dad and his father built a house on the west side of town overlooking the river. His father and mother are buried in the Brandenburg Cemetery. The town is dominated by the East and West Hills and sits in a depression on the river. These hills rise above the town and the Indiana landscape across the river. The only place to cross at this point is located at "downtown" Brandenburg. We can remember as youngsters — before the bridge was built — exploring a park at the river's edge and crossing the river by ferry at Brandenburg.*

The main force camped at Garnettsville, Kentucky, on the evening of July 7th. On the next morning they entered Brandenburg.

In the meantime, the Federal pursuit of Morgan was in full swing. General James Shakelford (starting from Russelville, Kentucky) and General Hobson (starting from Columbia) were fast on Morgan's trail.

Shakelford and Hobson's first thought was that Morgan would drive westward and then circle back to the South. When they arrived in Bardstown after Morgan had left they believed that he would soon begin his southern turn. They were surprised when Morgan made his sudden move toward the Ohio River and began to cross. They arrived too late to catch Morgan at Brandenburg.

# WILLIAM WOODROW SLIDER

## 7 CROSSING AT BRANDENBURG

On the morning of July 8, 1863, between 9:00 and 10:00 o'clock, General John Hunt Morgan arrived in Brandenburg, Kentucky, on the banks of the Ohio River. The reported arrival of the Confederates into the town is very colorful.

A group of officers went into E.C. Ashcraft's hotel and rolled three barrels of whiskey outside onto the sidewalk. One of the Sons of Dixie with an axe burst in the heads of the casks and invited his comrades to have a drink. Soldiers in passing would stop long enough to fill their canteens and continue.

A lady, Miss Carrie Doyle, was teaching music. One of Morgan's men climbed onto the piano and walked back and forth across the keys. (Boling, *Meade County Messenger*)

The relaxation and revelry were short, however, for across the river, the Indiana militia, augmented with some regulars, had already begun to assemble. General Morgan and his staff rode to the home of Robert Buckner on the West Hill of Brandenburg and there made their headquarters. Two of their artillery pieces were placed on the hill in a pasture, and two Parrott rifles were pulled to the East Hill and mounted in a yard of what was then the courthouse.

*Editors' Note: The Parrot Rifle was an artillery piece invented by Robert Parker Parrott. It was actually an advance in technology that included a rifled barrel and a reinforcing band that created a particularly accurate and inexpensive – though relatively unsafe – weapon. Parrott Rifled came in various sizes – from ten pounders to 300 pounders. Ten and twenty pound Parrott Rifles had ranges up to 5,000 yards and weighed up to 1,800 pounds.*

On the Indiana side, Colonel John Timberlake had about 300 men. He shouted across the river, "Shut down the steam on the McCombs and send over the steamer Alice Dean or I will blow you to Hades in five minutes." (Boling, *Meade County Messenger*)

During the previous night the Indiana Home Guard brought had brought an old cannon and unlimbered it on the bluff across from Brandenburg. Morgan immediately started using the *Dean* and the *McCombs* to ferry his men, horses, and artillery across the river. As the *McCombs* made its first trip across the Union forces in Indiana fired their cannon at the *Dean*. Three shots were wide of their mark; but one shot – the first – tore through the upper rigging of the *McCombs* wounding W.W. Wilson, quartermaster for the Confederates 1st Brigade, and scattering several cavalrymen.

Morgan's Parrott rifles quickly answered. Three rounds hit a cabin near the Hoosier cannon and silenced one gun. The small force of Hoosiers retreated to some steep hills about a mile from the river. During the retreat, two of the Union soldiers sat down to rest for a moment on the end of a log. A Confederate shell struck the other end of the log and both of them, James Kern and Jerry Nance, were killed.

The crossing continued for the moment. As the small Federal force retreated, the southerners began to gain the opposite bank. The 2nd Kentucky and the 9th Tennessee left their horses and boarded the steamers that placed them in Indiana. Here they skirmished for a moment and then their advance toward the bluffs.

Morgan watched the developments from the Brandenburg bluffs. He was apprehensive because two of his regiments now on the Indiana side of the river were on foot. Their horses were still on the Kentucky side.

The crossing was halted when the small Union gunboat *Springfield* arrived. The Union sailors fired three rounds into town; one into the Meade Hotel, one into the dock – killing two horses – and the third fell short of the *Dean* that was then in the middle of the Ohio River. Once more Morgan's Parrott rifles fired on the *Springfield* for an hour. Colonel Duke writes:

> *Suddenly checking her way, [the Springfield] tossed her snub nose defiantly like an angry beauty of the coal pits, sidled a little toward the town, and commenced to scold. A bluish-white funnel-shaped cloud sprouted out from her left hand bow and a shot*

*flew at the town, and then changing front forward she snapped a shell at the men on the other side.* (Duke, p433)

The Parrott guns immediately opened up on the gunboat and a dual ensued. Morgan watched the engagement with a show of emotion that he rarely exhibited. In his dangerous position he was separated by nearly one thousand feet of water from two of his best regiments. Behind him the pursuit was fast closing up. (Holland, p233) It was a very tense moment for the leader of the cavalry force and one of the most trying of the entire raid. The river was the nemesis that finally brought about Morgan's undoing a few days later.

The crossing stopped for an hour and a half, but eventually, the gunboat – its ammunition exhausted – retired upstream toward New Albany, Indiana. Ensign Joseph Watson, captain of the Springfield gives this report of the action:

*USS Springfield*
*Off New Albany*
*July 9, 1863*

Sir:
I engaged John H. Morgan this morning at nine o'clock at Brandenburg. I have been fighting nearly all day. He is crossing over to Indiana. He has 10,000 men and his batteries planted at three places commanding the river. We will have to have boats below town to operate with me. He wants to hold that place until he recrosses.

Joseph Watson

> *Acting Ensign, Commanding*
> *Lieutenant-Commander LeRoy Fitch*
> *No. 5, East Front* (ORN, Series II, Volume 1, p213)

*Author's note:* The gunboat USS *Springfield* is listed by the Navy Department as follows: Cost - $13,000.00; Class – Sternwheel steamer; Tonnage – 146; Engines – 2; Boilers – 2; Battery – January 8, 1863 – 6, 24 pdr. Howitzers; Speed – Upstream 5 miles; Length – 134' 9"; Beam – 26' 11"; Depth – 4' 4"; Name changed from *W.A. Healy*. (ORN, Series III, volume 3, p246)

After the *Springfield* withdrew, the horses were ferried across. Late in the afternoon, the gunboat returned with two transports of infantry )about 500 men) from Louisville.

Again a gun battle ensued. A citizen of Brandenburg described the havoc in the city as a result of the bombardment:

> *A shell from the gunboats [sic] went through Judge Perciful's kitchen, struck the stable at the old jail, and buried itself in the hill.... Another shell struck the Hotel Meade and went down through the building to the lower floor.... Another shell struck on the levee wounding one of the Confederates and killing two horses, and still another shattered a tree in front of a building on the main street.* (Boling, Meade County Messenger article)

Once more the *Springfield* was driven off by Morgan's Parrott rifles. The crossing took nearly seventeen hours.

It was dark before the first brigade had crossed and after midnight when the artillery was finally ferried over. The *Alice Dean* was then burned, since she was in government service, and the *McCombs* was released.

Once across, Morgan marched toward Corydon, meeting little resistance from the Indiana Home Guard. It would be a different story in Corydon, where the Hoosiers planned a warm reception for the Confederates.

On the first evening Morgan's force penetrated six miles into Indiana and camped at Frakes Mill. The people in the area had left their homes at a moment's notice and the suppers in many places were still on the tables as the Confederates advanced.

# 8 THROUGH INDIANA

On July 9, 1863 General John Hunt Morgan started his raiders for Corydon, Indiana, having crossed the Ohio River at nearby Brandenburg, Kentucky  The Union forces were in an uproar.

The Battle of Corydon

*Columbus, Indiana*
*July 8, 1863*
*Please, let me know what naval force you have to meet Morgan.*
*Asboth, Brigadier General*

*Cairo, Illinois*
*July 9, 1863*
*We have six gunboats on the Ohio, and will send others, if possible. At what point did Morgan cross, and where is it probably he will attempt to recross?*
*A.M. Pennock,*
*Fleet Captain and Commandant of the Station*
*Governor Morton*
*Indianapolis, Indiana*
*(ORN, p483)*

Governor Oliver P. Morton worked feverishly to organize Indiana's defense, calling for able-bodied men to take up arms and form militia companies. Thousands of men responded and organized themselves into companies and regiments. Colonel Lewis Jordan took command of the 450 members of the Harrison County Home Guard (the 6th Regiment of the Indiana Legion). This command consisted of poorly trained civilians with a motley collection of arms. Colonel Jordan's goal was to delay Morgan long enough for Union reinforcements to arrive. (*HHHills.org*)

Morgan's second brigade took the advance up the narrow, dusty Maukport Road that led to Corydon, some fifteen miles from the river. The lead elements were led by Colonel Richard Morgan.

The advance guard came upon a group of Colonel Jordan's Union militia posted just one mile south of the town. They were behind breastworks made of logs and fence rails; and they defended their position with resolve.

General Morgan then extended his flanks and forced the defenders to retreat toward the town. This action – lasting less than one hour – constituted the only battle in the Civil War on Indiana soil.

Accounts vary as to the number of casualties of the Battle of Corydon, but the most reliable evidence suggests that four of Jordan's men were killed, ten to twelve were wounded, and 355 were captured. Morgan counted eleven dead and forty wounded raiders. Among the dead Federals was the civilian toll keeper who perished near his tollgate. Raiders killed a Lutheran minister on his farm, four miles from the battlefield and stole horses from several other farmers. Also, among the wounded was Morgan's adjutant, Lieutenant Thorpe, of Company "A" of the Second Kentucky Cavalry.

General Morgan led his division into Corydon, where he paroled his demoralized prisoners and ransomed the town for cash and supplies. In the town, Morgan stopped at the Corydon Hotel. Here the daughter of the innkeeper informed the general of Lee's defeat at Gettysburg. Morgan was dismayed. The apparent objective of his great raid – to join the victorious General Lee – had disappeared, but there was no turning back now. The advance continued. That night the cavalry camped on the road eighteen miles from Salem, Indiana.

Meanwhile, back at Brandenburg, the pursuit was gathering. Union forces were coming down the river and across land from the south. Morgan's immediate avenue of retreat was closed.

> *USS Moose*
> *Off Brandenburg, Kentucky*
> *July 9th, 1863*
> *I arrived here between 5 and 6pm and much to my disappointment and sorrow, found the enemy had effected a crossing by means of the two steamers captured. On my arrival here I found General Hobson's forces coming into the town, following General Morgan. I hope with the aid of the merchant steamers, he will have his entire force across the river before mid-night and after Morgan.*
> *Leroy Fitch*
> *Lieutenant Commander*
> *(ORN, p483)*

General Hobson was thus close upon the heels of the Confederates. Riding into Brandenburg, the Union cavalry established headquarters in the Methodist Church and rested for a while.

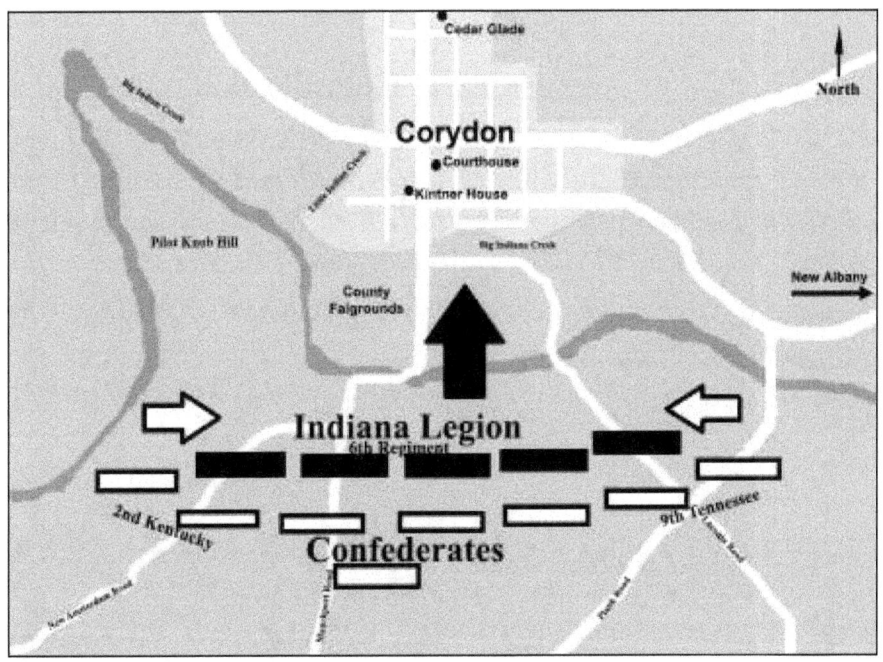

*Editors' note: The author, William W. Slider was serving as pastor of the Brandenburg Methodist Church when he wrote this work. We recall him speaking of the bullet holes that were in the front doors of the church which, as legend had it, were errant shots from the skirmish in Brandenburg.*

Maj. Gen. Ambrose Burnside, commander of the Department of the Ohio with headquarters in Cincinnati, Ohio, quickly organized local Federal troops and home militia to cut off Morgan's routes back to the South. (*HHHills.org*) With Morgan almost half way through the state of Indiana, however, the union defense and pursuit seemed to falter.

*Editors' Note: The 1956 movie,* **Friendly Persuasion,** *is a depiction of a Quaker family in southern Indiana during the Civil War. The movie stars Gary Cooper, Dorothy McGuire, and Anthony Perkins. The movie deals with important social issues during the Civil War in a humorous manner. The last part of the movie is a fictional, but accurate portrayal of the panic created by Morgan's raid into southern Indiana and the response of the citizenry.*

> *Indianapolis, July 10, 1863*
> *Secretary of War:*
> *Quartermaster here has telegraphed Quartermaster-General for authority to turn over to the State of Indiana uniforms for Indiana Legion, called out to repel invasion and can get no answer. Please order the issue at once. Troops are being rapidly organized, and many are not ready to move. Answer.*
>
> *O.P. Morton*
> *Governor of Indiana*
> *(Official Records, Series III, Volume 3, p481)*

From Ohio, where Morgan was headed, came this plea:

> *Columbus, Ohio, July 11, 1863*
> *Hon. E.M. Stanton:*
> *Please authorize me to issue arms to the volunteer militia of Ohio for border defense. You have about 15,000 stands of arms in our arsenal unfit for service in the field.*
>
> *David Tod*
> *Governor*
> *(Official Records, Series III, Volume 3, p483)*

Numerous dispatches of like nature flew between the governors and the War Department. Meanwhile, Morgan, unhampered by the bureaucratic process, with no supply base to defend, living on the country through which he passed, and with no definite point toward which he must journey, was playing havoc with peace and order in the sovereign states of Indiana and Ohio.

*Editors' note: General Morgan's advance into Indiana was more than just an annoyance or even a propaganda ploy. Across the river from Louisville, in Jeffersonville, Indiana, was a large Federal supply depot. Both editors are familiar with this large site, which they passed numerous times during the 1970s on the way from Louisville to Hanover College in Indiana.*

In one field, Morgan was making hay – that of prisoners. In a letter from the Secretary of War to the President there is a complaint that a considerable number represented as prisoners were not soldiers, but were non-combatants – citizens of towns and villages, farmers, travelers, and others in civilian life not captured in battle, but taken in their homes, on their farms, or on the highways by General Morgan and his raiders, who put them under a "sham" parole. The Secretary objected that to use these prisoners in exchange for Confederate soldiers taken in the field would be relieving the enemy from the pressure of war a would enable him to protract the conflict. (*Official Records, Series III, volume 3, p1130*)

On the morning of the 10th of July the confederate troops began a march toward Salem, Indiana, following three parallel routes. Major Weber took the advance with Lieutenant Welsh and Company K riding the point with twelve men.

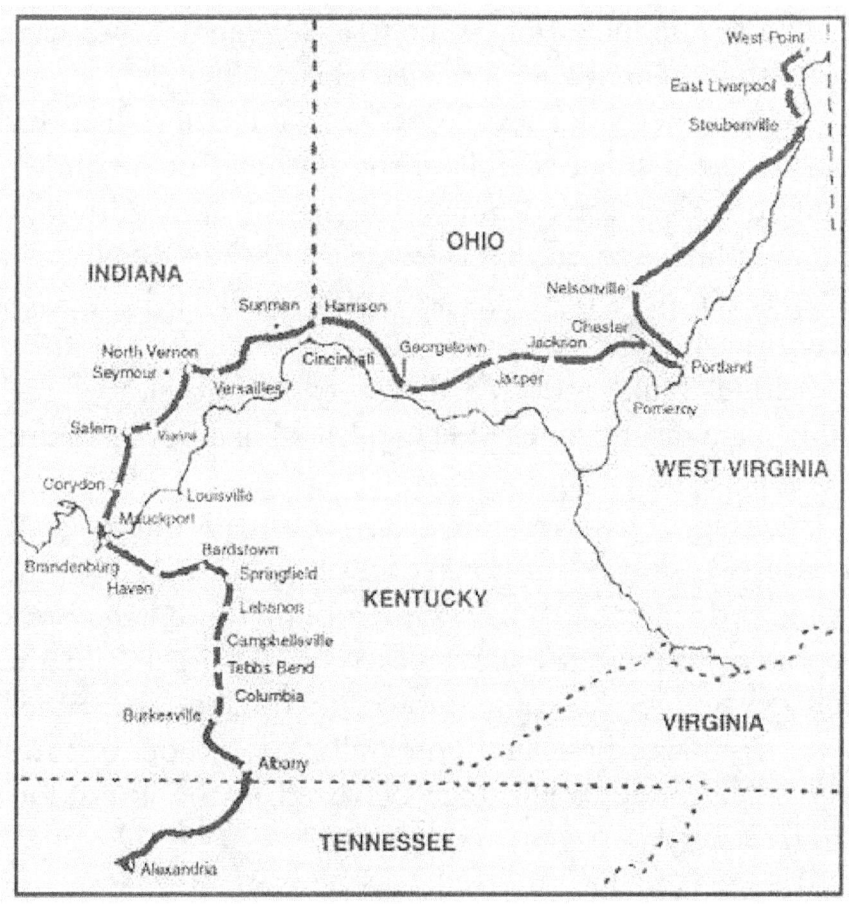

Just outside Salem about 150 Hoosiers had gathered to resist the invasion. Lieutenant Welsh charged them and they scattered toward the town. The pursuit continued into the town where it was discovered that two or three hundred citizens were being armed. With a few random shots the Confederates entered Salem.

Although General Morgan had appointed Major Steele the Provost Marshal of his raiders, he was unable – even with the help of the officers – to stop the looting of Salem that started. Calico seemed to the article sought more than any other, though some soldiers took their looting to the ludicrous. One man liberated a bird cage with three canaries and carried on the march for two days. Another soldier rode off with a chafing dish that looked like a small coffin on the pommel of his saddle until an officer forced him to throw it away. Although the weather was intensely warm, another cavalryman slung seven pairs of skates around his neck and chuckled over his acquisition.

Colonel Duke reported that very few articles of real value were taken. The soldiers pillaged like boys robbing an orchard. (*Duke, p.437*)

Entering Salem the next day, Morgan immediately took possession of the town and placed guards over the stores and streets. His cavalrymen burned the large brick depot, along with all the railcars on the track and the railroad bridges on each side of town. They demanded taxes from area flour and grist mills. After looting stores and taking about $500, they departed in the afternoon. (*HHHills.org*)

Morgan and his troops left Salem about 2:00pm on July 10th and moved rapidly toward Vienna, where they arrived after dusk. Here they burned a railroad bridge and depot. (*HHHills.org*)

Morgan had decided to advance roughly parallel to the river. Had he turned north, he might well have captured Indianapolis and freed 3,000 Confederate prisoners before General Lew Wallace, who had been summoned from leave, could form a defense.

At Vienna, Ellsworth tapped the telegraph lines and learned that the raiders were safe for the moment. They proceeded to Lexington, Indiana, some five miles away, and rested for the night. That night Federal cavalry rode into the town – even to the house where Morgan was sleeping – but suddenly and inexplicably left.

Early the next morning, Morgan sent Colonel Smith to make a feint at Madison, Indiana. The ruse worked. The Union leaders believed that Morgan would attempt to re-cross the Ohio River at Madison.

> *July 11, 1863 – 12:30pm*
> *Dispatch Received. Morgan is now supposed to be not far from Vernon. He may attempt to cross above Madison, or he may turn and try to cross below Louisville. I will try to communicate to you all the information I get of his movements by telegraph.*
> 
> *A.E. Burnside,*
> *Major General*
> 
> *LeRoy Fitch*
> *Gunboat Moose, New Albany*
> *(ORN, p 249)*

Morgan probably never learned that large numbers of Confederates were trying to join with him on July 11th, but could not reach him. LeRoy Fitch, who hung doggedly to Morgan's heels through the raid says, "The whole river appears to be infested with guerrillas all at once. I am now in great hopes of being able to meet Morgan."

Whether or not these additional recruits would have made any great contribution to the tiring cavalry is hard to say. Evidently Morgan's troops were well-prepared to carry the war to the North.

> *Madison, Indiana*
> *July 12, 1863*
> *Sir: In my letter of yesterday I mentioned the Springfield and Victory having cut off reinforcements attempting to cross the river to join Morgan. This force, as I learned today, amounted to 1,500; 45, as I mentioned before, succeeded in getting over; some few it is reported were drowned, and 39 were held on the island and taken prisoners by the infantry forces coming up on transports after the gunboats; 50 horses were also captured.*
> *Very respectfully, your obedient servant*
> *Leroy Fitch*
> *Lieutenant Commander*
> *Acting Rear Admiral David C. Porter*
> *Commanding Mississippi Squadron*

(ORN, p249)

*Author's Note: The island of which Admiral Porter wrote was Twelve Mile Island above Louisville.*

Morgan's troops moved on toward Vernon, which they sighted by afternoon. Here Smith rejoined the main force, unaware that at Madison he had been within gunshot of 1,500 mounted Confederates trying to join him.

Morgan sent a demand for the surrender of Vernon, but was answered by General Love, who requested that he be allowed to remove non-combatants. Love reported in a hasty dispatch:

> *Vernon, 12th*
>
> *Arrived here last night in time to answer Morgan's second demand for surrender. Sent him word our force was sufficient to hold the town. He said thirty minutes would open his artillery. God the women and children out as fast as possible and made the best disposition possible with our force and limited time. Expected attack every minute until 2 o'clock when information I believe to be reliable leads me to believe he declines a fight, and is hastening towards Madison. If so he will reach the Ohio at Madison, or vicinity, about early dawn. I don't think he can escape, Information looks as if his command was wearied out [sic] and he [is] anxious about his escape.*
>
> *Love, General*

**(ORN p418)**

General Morgan settled for burning a bridge in Vernon, and moved onto Dupont, Indiana. In Dupont a meat-packing plant engaged the attention of the raiders and nearly all of the Confederates had a ham tied to their saddle.

More than hams were being captured by Morgan's men; for by this time they were averaging twenty hours in the saddle per day and the pursuit of General Hobson was so intense that the raiders had to change horses often. The Federals, close on their heels, simply recaptured the horses that were abandoned by the Confederates.

This haphazard practice of requisitioning horses caused much confusion in the settlement of war claims. The commissioners appointed to settle the damages associated with the Morgan Raid were swamped with thousands of claims – some extremely insignificant, such as a claim for a bowie knife valued at $1.25, and another claim for two sacks of apples valued a two dollars. (*Holland, p268*). The Ohio Claims Commission paid about $500,000 for damages by the Confederates and $200,000 for damages by their Union pursuers.

It may be appropriate to mention at this point that there were two opposite opinions of Morgan among the Unionists. One opinion was that Morgan was urging his men to every conceivable excess. The other opinion believed that Morgan was considerate of the rights of the people of Ohio and Indiana as any raiders were on either side under like circumstances. (*Holland, p239*)

In Versailles a group of freebooters invaded the local Masonic Lodge and lifted the lodge's silver coin jewelry. General Morgan, himself a Mason, ordered the jewels returned, punishing the thievery of his own men. (*HHHills.org*) A bridge was burned near Versailles.

General Morgan continued to press on toward Sunman, Indiana, located on the Ohio and Mississippi Railroad. At Sunman the raiders rested almost within sight of 2,500 Indiana militia loaded entrained on boxcars headed for Cincinnati – they were unaware that Morgan was in the area.

At 5:00 A.M. Morgan resumed his march toward the Indiana-Ohio border. They crossed into Ohio in the early morning of July 13, 1863.

## 9 THE END IN OHIO

At 10:00 o'clock in the morning of July 13th, Morgan's Raiders reached Harrison, Ohio – just across the Indiana-Ohio border. As Morgan entered Ohio, the pursuing forces lost him for a time.

*USS Moose*
*Aurora, Indiana*
*July 13, 1863*
*Sir: Since my second letter of the 11th, I have been following up the river trying to keep on Morgan's right, as it is reported he is moving to the northward and eastward. At last accounts he was making to strike the river at this point, but he is now reported to be 15 miles back and making still to the north. It seems almost impossible to get any positive*

*information as to his exact location or movements, etc.*

*LeRoy Fitch*
*Lieutenant Commander*

*Acting Rear Admiral David D. Porter,*
*Commanding Mississippi Squadron*
(Navy Department p251)

As Morgan pounded on, deep into enemy territory, he realized the box into which he had placed himself – albeit, not unwittingly. His strategy was to maneuver outside Cincinnati where he expected to be met by the forces of generals Burnside and Judah. He had formulated no particular plan for meeting them, but hoped to elude them, since he realized that it would be a superhuman task to cut his way through them. He realized, also, that the cavalry hanging to his rear could not overtake him if he kept moving.

On the night of July 12th, Ohio Governor David Tod issued a proclamation calling out the Ohio militia to protect the southern counties from Morgan's Raiders. Many militiamen, however, did not hear of the proclamation in a timely manner. (www.OhioHistoryCentral.org)

Morgan believed that the transportation of troops by river would be impeded by the falling of the river. He also believed that there would be a general effort to catch him as he crossed the road leading from Hamilton to Dayton, Ohio. He, therefore, set about deceiving the Union generals as to when and where he would cross this road. His small decoy parties dispersed in all directions from Harrison in order to add confusion, but pointed in the general direction of Hamilton.

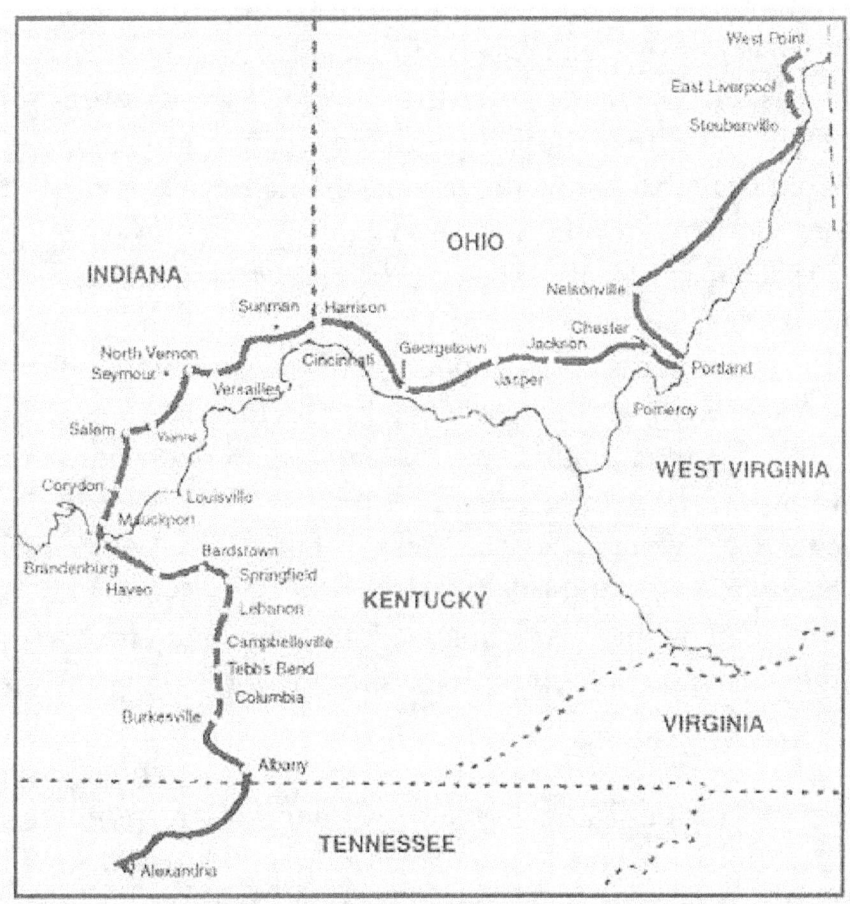

Some of Morgan's men, those lagging behind or wounded, tried to cross from Indiana to Kentucky at the time Morgan was planning his way past Cincinnati. A dispatch, dated July 13th, states that the gunboats *Springfield* and *Victory* fell in with a portion of Morgan's men trying to cross at Twelve Mile Island (near Louisville, Kentucky). These Confederate stragglers were driven back except for a few that had already crossed. The remainder fled with Union cavalry in hot pursuit.

After two or three hours at Harrison, Ohio, Morgan felt that he was ready to continue. He was certain that his maneuvers had drawn the bulk of Union forces up the road and that the enemy that remained in Cincinnati would draw back into the city on the defensive instead of attempting to stop him.

Morgan is often criticized for not entering Cincinnati, but it must be remembered that he had not the vaguest idea of its defense, had ridden fifty miles the day before to reach the city, arrived at nightfall, and had less than 2,000 effectives at this time. Morgan had determined to move across Ohio. To return to Kentucky from Cincinnati would have admitted failure to reach this objective. In addition crossing back into Kentucky at Cincinnati would have released the pursuing forces to other activities including harassing General Bragg in his retreat.

Morgan called for two men who knew Cincinnati, and two of President Zachary Taylor's nephews responded – Captain Taylor and Lieutenant McLain. These two men entered the city and returned with reports of great turmoil and excitement. Cincinnati was under martial law and all the men were flocking to the defense. Morgan's problem now was to get around this defended city.

The march continued with General Morgan in the advance, followed by Colonel Johnson's brigade and then Colonel Duke's. Officers had to ride up and down the line shouting for the men to close ranks. Weary and saddle-worn, they straggled along the road. Many fell from their horses and slept by the road until awakened by a Union bayonet prodding them. The regiment of Colonel Cluke was at the rear of Johnson's brigade, and its rear companies began to lose ground, thus putting gap between themselves and the rest of the column. As the march continued, the gap grew. Thus Colonel Duke's brigade lost contact with the lead brigade and had to resort to reading signposts and hoof prints on the road in order to follow the rest of the corps.

*Editors' Note: Movement in column is extremely difficult to maintain. Even in well-rested or mechanized troops, those at the end of a column will have difficulty maintaining contact even though the lead elements maintain a constant pace. The trail elements tend to "accordion" – crowding forward, then slowing, then falling back, then hurrying to make contact. Movement in column has the benefit of being simple to control, but it does put a burden on following elements – especially if they are tired.*

Colonel Adam Johnson, weary as the rest, sat on his horse at an intersection, checking off the regiments of his brigade as they passed. Colonel Cluke rode up to him, his clothes and beard flaked with dust and his eyes heavy from loss of sleep. "I'd give a thousand dollars for an hour of sleep," he muttered. Johnson held the reins of Cluke's horse while the regimental commander slept for an hour in his saddle. It is probable that Colonel Johnson did not demand payment of the one thousand dollars. (*Holland, p243*)

Major Steele went forward to drive the pickets and scouts. His select body of men did a thorough job. To advance through an unfamiliar town, filled with enemy troops, deep in enemy territory at night is no mean achievement, and the job assigned to the Major was one of the most difficult of the raid.

Skirting Cincinnati, the command rode to the east. At one time they marched through Glendale – a suburb of Cincinnati – and crossed every principal road. After stopping for a few minutes to destroy some track of the Little Miami Railroad, they moved on and rested in sight of Camp Dennison. The raiders skirmished here and burned some Union government wagons as daylight broke.

After another grueling day of riding by 4:00 P.M. the Confederate column was in Williamsburg, Ohio – twenty-eight miles from Cincinnati. It was an amazing ride. Since leaving Sunman, Indiana, in a period of thirty-five hours, Morgan's soldiers had ridden more than ninety miles – the greatest march that even Morgan had made. (*Young, p386*).

After a night of rest the entire command was in better spirits. On the morning of July 15th, Morgan responded to Colonel Johnson, who was seeking orders, "All our troubles are now over. The river is only twenty-five miles away and tomorrow we will be on southern soil." (Duke, p444).

The Federals thought differently:

> *New Albany, July 14, 1863*
> *(received 15th)*
> *Naumkeag over the shoals. Will want her here for patrol above Louisville for a few days. Do not think Morgan can escape. Have seven boats on patrol from Madison to Carrollton. Had five boats at Brandenburg 9th, be he had gone.*
> *Leroy Fitch*
> *Lieutenant Commander*
> (ORN, p251)

In forty-eight hours the Ohio had risen one foot; the river was rising rapidly. Morgan's line of march went through Georgetown – about twelve miles from the river, but the high water and the gunboats turned the Confederate column toward fords at Buffington Island – about ninety miles to the east. The militia was very active now. They felled trees, burned bridges, sniped at the column, and impeded progress in every possible way.

The situation grew more intense. The Union leaders sensed the goal of Morgan's dash from Georgetown.

> *July 16, 1863*
> *I trust you to check the enemy at Pomeroy and Buffington Island until our men get up. There is a force of our men and two pieces of artillery at Buffington. I am sure you will not allow them to cross if you can prevent it.*
>
> *A.E. Burnside*
> *Major General*
> (ORN)

The eyes of the North and South alike were focused on Morgan. The North was amazed at his daring march and elusive methods; the South pinned its waning hope on the dashing cavalryman. Vicksburg had fallen on July 4th and, rapidly upon its heels, Gettysburg had ended disastrously for the Confederacy. General Bragg was falling back in Tennessee. Morgan's was the only remaining offensive the South had.

The Richmond Enquirer on July 16th, 1863, stated:

> *This bold raid is the only actively aggressive operation in which our forces are engaged. It is the only real movement we are making toward a restoration of peace. Peace must be conquered on the enemy's ground, or it will not come at all.*

The pressure on Morgan increased, and as the Confederate column swept by Pomeroy on the 18th of July, the Federals were carrying out Burnside's orders with will. Colonel Duke says that in passing near Pomeroy there was one continual fight.

Morgan was growing weary and alarmed. Any hope of assistance from Copperheads in Ohio had not materialized. The ride had been grueling. The men were reaching the end of their endurance. Any suitable ford was still far away. The Chicago Tribune on July 18th, 1863 best describes Morgan's predicament: "John Morgan is still in Ohio, or rather is in Ohio without being allowed to be still."

Morgan could not afford to be still. He tried to rest his men at Chester, Ohio, at one o'clock in the afternoon. The one and one-half hours they spent there brought the raiders to Buffington Island after dark.

This late arrival was a tragic turn of events for Morgan. It required the cavalry to assault an union defensive position in the dark if they were to escape to the opposite shore. The exact position of the defense was not known, and even the terrain itself was unfamiliar to the Southerners. Morgan had no means for knowing how many troops the federals had guarding two fords, nor their positions.

Morgan had to make his plans for attack with haste, yet with as much certainty as possible. This critical time waiting on the northern bank of the Ohio River must have at least called a fleeting remembrance to Morgan's mind of the time at Brandenburg, Kentucky – only a few days ago – when he stood on the southern shore and looked hopefully northward.

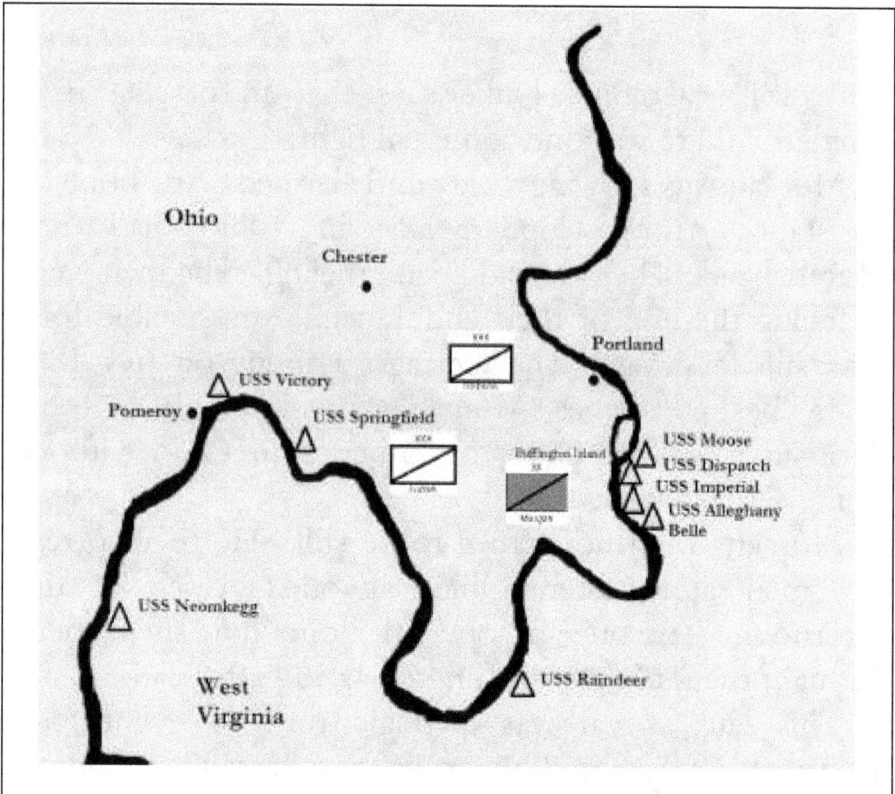

The "box" in which Morgan placed himself on the evening of July 18th, 1863. US Navy gunboats are shown with triangles.

Morgan held a council of war. Someone suggested that by leaving the wounded, artillery, and wagons the crossing could be made at a deeper ford up river. Morgan rejected this idea and decided to take all or lose all.

Two regiments were ordered to place themselves ready for the assault on the Federal position at dawn. Soon they were ready. It was here that the entire success of the raid hung in the balance, and about 2:00 A.M. the scale tipped against the Southern side. Weary

Confederate scouts failed to detect the abandonment of the Union positions. The ford was undefended! Had Morgan had this information, he could have moved his entire force across the river before the enemy could stop them.

When dawn came on July 19th and the discovery was made, Colonel Duke immediately moved a force up the Pomeroy Road a few miles to pursue the retreating Union soldiers. This pursuing force stumbled upon General Judah's advance guard and learned that his cavalry was only a short distance away with about 8,000 riders.

Here began on of the most magnificent cavalry battles in history – the Battle of Buffington Island – the largest battle of the Civil War in Ohio. On the one side were the sons of Michigan and Indiana; and on the other side were the boys of Kentucky and Tennessee.

The 5th and 6th Kentucky Calvary Regiments formed to meet the charge of the Union forces – the first wave of the 7th and 8th Michigan and the 5th Indiana. The charge was turned, but only after a portion of the 5th Kentucky was cut off and their Parrott rifles captured.

The blue line reformed for a second charge. Colonel Duke sent hurriedly to General Morgan for the 2nd Kentucky.

Firing began in the rear of the Confederates who were facing toward the river. Couriers from Colonel Johnson informed Colonel Duke that Union cavalry under General Hobson was attacking. Unaware of the presence of each other, generals Hobson and Judah had by accident caught the Confederates in a box or *cul de sac*.

Along the river Union gunboats began to fire. Morgan was trapped.

The US Navy's Mississippi Squadron was involved in Battle of Buffington Island. The US Navy had been involved in the chase ever since General Morgan had crossed the Ohio River at Brandenburg.

Lieutenant Commander Leroy Fitch's fleet included several tinclads and ironclads. Fitch established a "zone defense" along the Ohio River. The US Army's "amphibious division" officer, Major General Ambrose E. Burnside at his Cincinnati headquarters, provided intelligence of Morgan's march and turned his flagship, *Alleghany Belle*, over to Fitch before the battle. The "amphibious division's" tinclads had four to six large johnboats (side boats) used as platforms for firing rifles, for landing to give chase and pickup prisoners. Fitch's flagship was the ironclad USS *Moose*.

The dispatch privateer, *Imperial*, was tied up within earshot of the island the night before the battle. It has been written that Fitch had the boilers fired up and shooting its large cannons at the island on first rifle fire, slightly out of range before steam could make way. *Allegheny Belle* was a little farther down tied up along the Ohio side. Having heard *Moose*'s cannons, it made steam and soon brought up Burnsides' amphibious infantry.

Continuing upstream after the main battle began, the USS *Moose* fired on a Confederate Artillery column trying to cross the river above the island at the next shoal crossing. Fitch dispatched *Imperial* to recover Confederate field artillery left behind there.

General Morgan turned his force to oppose the Union forces on land. Colonels Johnson and Duke placed their brigades at right angles. Johnson was opposite Hobson, and Duke opposed Judah. General Judah formed a line of infantry in his front and sent the Michigan cavalry as skirmishers on a ridge to the right. This deployment put the entire Confederate force under a crossfire. To the rear (if there could be a direction considered the rear in all of the confusion) General Morgan was attempting to draw off the 2nd and 9th Tennessee and the 8th and 11th Kentucky. Colonel Duke tells the story:

> *The scene in the rear of the lines engaged was one of indescribable confusion. While the bulk of the regiments which General Morgan was drawing off were moving from the field in perfect order, there were many stragglers from each who were circling about the valley in a delirium of fright, clinging instinctively in their terror to bolts of calico and holding on to [other trinkets], but changing the direction in which they galloped with every shell which whizzed or burst near them. The long train of wagons and ambulances dashed wildly in the only direction which promised escape, and becoming locked and entangled with each other in their flight, many were upset and terrified horses broke loose from them and plunged wildly through the mass. Some of them in striving to make their way out of the valley at the northern end, ran afoul of the howitzers attached to the 2nd Brigade, and guns and wagons were rolling headlong into the steep ravine. Occasionally, a solid shot or*

*shell would strike one and bowl it over like a tumbled ten pin.* (Duke, p453)

Duke and Johnson began to fall back toward the river. There were only two ways to escape from the box – two ravines – that were immediately jammed with men and equipment. The gunboats fired into the ravines, and the 7th Michigan attacked. Colonel Duke with 700 men and officers surrendered.

General Morgan continued with the remnant northward up the Chester Road. He tried to cross the river again about twenty miles above Buffington Island, and 300 men under Johnson got across. Morgan, in midstream turned back to Ohio when he saw the entire remnant could not make it.

*Editors' Note: General Morgan did not file an after action report, and the Union commanders had only their perspective to report.*

The indefatigable Lt. Commander Fitch tells the story:

*USS Moose*
*Above Buffington Island*
*Ohio River*
*July 19th, 1863*
*After chasing Morgan nearly 500 miles, I at last met him on the river at this point. I engaged and drove him back capturing two pieces of artillery. He abandoned rest to General Judah His forces broke in confusion from the banks, and left his wagon train, many horses and small arms in my possession.*

> *General Judah is now in pursuit of the remnant of his forces.*
>
> *LeRoy Fitch*
> *Lieutenant Commander, US Navy*
> *Rear Admiral D.D. Porter*
> *Commanding Mississippi Squadron, Vicksburg*
> *(ORN, p254)*

Morgan returned to his men on the Ohio side of the river and found that his command had dwindled to about 800 men. Both of his brigade commanders were gone – Duke was captured, and Johnson had escaped. Morgan formed two provisional brigades under Cluke and Weber commanding.

The march continued. They forded small rivers and climbed tall hills, constantly calling on what little strength was left. On July 26th the 2nd Kentucky's "C" Company made the last charge.

The charge left Morgan 250 men He determined to surrender on terms, for he realized the Battle of Gettysburg would result in swarms of prisoners which in turn would lessen the opportunity for parole. He, therefore, determined to surrender on terms in at all possible. He approached a Captain Burbeck of the Ohio militia. He agreed to leave Burbeck's district unmolested if the captain would lead him to the Pennsylvania border.

As they rode, Morgan saw a dust cloud in the distance – first behind them, then to the side, and then ahead. He knew that he was caught. He agreed to surrender to Burbeck on terms that the officers should keep their side arms and horses, and the men their horses. Almost immediately, General Shackelford, Hobson's second-in-command, arrived and refused the terms.

There has been considerable discussion of the refusal of terms. Morgan claims that he surrendered to a captain of the Ohio militia on terms which were rejected, but the Union side has a different story. General Shackelford says that he told Morgan "that the Union forces had followed him thirty days and nights; that his demand could not be considered a moment; that [he] regarded his surrender to the militia captain under such circumstances as not only absurd and ridiculous, but unfair and illegal, and that [he] would not recognize it at all." (*Speed, p236*)

General Morgan wrote to Governor Todd of Ohio to insist upon the rights of the terms of surrender. The governor replied, "Said Burbeck is not and never was a militia officer of the state. He was captured by you and traveled with you some considerable distance before your surrender. Burbeck himself says, "I was captain of no militia whatever, or any other force of men, but was appointed that Sunday morning as captain by the men that went out with me on horseback, there being some fifteen or twenty in number. (*ORA, Series 1, Volume XXIII, p814*)

## 10 RESULTS OF THE RAID

The Great Raid came to an end not far from the Pennsylvania border, near New Lisbon, Ohio. North and South, there was a great dispute as to whether the raid had accomplished anything.

It is true that General Bragg had been able to retreat without molestation from a flanking force. General Rosecrans was deprived of men who would have been present at Chickamauga, instead of being employed chasing Morgan.

In the *Chattanooga Times* of July 20th, 1883, J.E. McGowan observed, "Morgan's raid changed the whole aspect of military operations in Tennessee and Kentucky in the summer and fall of 1863; but for his delaying Burnside's movement ... that commander with 28,000 men would have joined Rosecrans three weeks before the Battle of Chickamauga was fought."

Most Northerners had the attitude that the raid, though colorful, was meaningless:

> *Nothing is shown by any reports to have been accomplished by the raid. What it was except a long ride ending in capture is not shown in any reports. No important place was touched and nothing was effected except the excitement incidental to such a passage through the country. Nor was it favorably commented on by the Confederate authorities.* (Speed, p233)

The citizenry of the Confederate States of America after the battles of Gettysburg, Vicksburg, and Tullahoma must have become resigned to defeats, and probably looked with both pride and resignation to Morgan's raid.

> *General Morgan like a comet has shot out of the beaten track of the army and after dashing deeply into Indiana the last heard of him he was in Ohio, near Cincinnati. He was playing havoc with the steamboats, and capturing fine horses. He has some 3,000 men we cannot afford to lose – but I fear they will be lost.* (Jones' Diary, July 20th, 1863)

General Bragg best summarizes the Confederate Army's consensus of the several raids by Morgan. Bragg wrote: "Should he ever return with his command it will as usual be disorganized and unfit for service until again armed, equipped, and disciplined." (*Speed, p239*)

Whether Morgan desired to surround his name with glory and make it immortal in military annals, or whether he struck out in a desire to carry the war to the North in any way, or whether it was the result of a well-studied plan, we cannot say with any certainty. Perhaps it was a bit of all three, although the last is doubtful in the light of events; but John Morgan's determination, zeal, and bravery tend to cause us to give him the benefit of the doubt. The subsequent actions of his command, which will be described in a latter chapter, reveal a spirit that indelibly impresses upon all readers of Morgan's story that the Great Raid was made, not for glory, but in the belief that it would aid the Confederacy by diverting large numbers of enemy troops. Morgan at least delayed the downfall of the Confederacy.

At various times and places during the raid there had been more than 100,000 men in pursuit of Morgan. Elements of the US Army, Navy, and even the Marine Corps had been detailed to bring him to bay. Morgan and his troops had ridden about 500 miles through the North and over 1,000 miles behind enemy lines.

Some assume that if Forrest had had Morgan's men that were lost in Ohio, and turned them loose on July 21st at the Battle of Chickamauga, there would have been a Confederate victory. They forget, however, that had Morgan been present at the battle, so in all likelihood would the 28,000 men that were drawn away from Burnside's forces by Morgan. In comparison to these numbers, General Morgan's 2,500 men would have provided a negligible contribution to that battle.

After the defeat of General Morgan the South never again effectively invaded Northern territory. Morgan had carried the war to the enemy and in so doing had buoyed the spirits of the Confederacy to a considerable degree, if only momentarily. There is no doubt that Morgan became an outstanding hero and source of inspiration to the Confederacy.

> *January 1, 1864 – The President had a reception today and the city councils have voted the hospitalities of the city to Brigadier General J.H. Morgan, whose arrival is expected. If he comes he will be the hero and have a larger crowd of admirers around him than the President.* (P. Jones, volume II, p122.)

It would be well, however, to give credit to both sides in this matter. If Morgan made a great ride, then the Northern troops under Shackelford and Hobson certainly did also. They followed the Confederates all the way from Burkesville, Kentucky, across the state, into Indiana, and across the state of Ohio. They at last out rode, turned upon the pursued, surrounded them, and captured them. It is claimed for Morgan that at one point he made ninety miles in thirty-five hours. What, then, must have been the riding capacity of the pursuers who succeeded in overtaking a force moving so rapidly? Indeed, the pursuit was more remarkable than the raid. (*Speed, pp237-8*)

## 11 THE END OF THE TRAIL

Brigadier General John Hunt Morgan and many of his men were confined in the state penitentiary at Columbus, Ohio. Much has been written and much more was said about this incarceration. It was bitterly denounced by the Confederates as a negation of the principles applying to the treatment of prisoners-of-war. The beards and hair of the men were shorn close, but this seems to be the greatest indignity that occurred. They were rigidly inspected on occasions, but even Colonel Duke gives no indication that the prisoners were mistreated. Many irritating and humiliating incidents occurred in the prison, but for the most part the men of Morgan's command agreed after the war that their treatment was not overly stern. Duke reports that food was sufficient, and books and writing materials were allowed.

*Author's Note: My grandfather, who was a prisoner of the Confederates a Andersonville and Libby, did not say the same about those camps.*

Morgan's men grew restless in prison following the news of the Confederate loss at the Battle of Chickamauga, and they determined to escape by any means possible. Captain Hines discovered that there was an air tunnel underneath the lower tier of cells and was prepared to dig himself out.

In order to carry out the operation, it was necessary that the men dig through the floor of a cell to the air passage, and then work from there. Knives from the dinner tables were used as tools and the hole in the cell floor was covered by a carelessly tossed carpet bag. The men then set to work on a tunnel toward the main wall and designed to come up just inside it. A rope was then thrown over the wall and the escape was thus completed.

On the night of November 26, 1863, Morgan along with Captain Hines and five others made good their escape. Morgan and Hines finally made their way to Athens, Tennessee. The general immediately set out for Richmond amid the ovations of the citizenry along the way. His reception from the Richmond officials was rather lukewarm. Only a portion of his old command could be restored to him. He finally took the field with two brigades – about 2,000 strong – to command the Department of Southwestern Virginia. Later Colonel Basil Duke and several others were exchanged and soon rejoined Morgan.

Here also should be mentioned that the remnant that had escaped at Buffington Island with Colonel Adam

Johnson had marched through the mountains of West Virginia and finally to the vicinity of Knoxville. In Knoxville this remnant reformed under Johnson and was present at the Battle of Chickamauga.

In June of 1864 Morgan was again raiding in Kentucky. On July 8th Morgan's force reached Mount Sterling. General Morgan left a detachment in Mount Sterling and took the main body to Lexington.

At about 3:00 o'clock on the morning of June 9th, Union forces encountered Morgan's force in Mount Sterling. The Confederate Lieutenant Headley reports, "The enemy was coming into camp now, shooting men as they got up or as they lay asleep. It looked like a slaughter." (*P. Headley, p189*)

Colonel Duke, who was not present, says that the pickets gave no warning and the trap was sprung by the Federals. The pickets were so surprised that they ran through the camp yelling the alarm. (*P. Headley, p198*)

The Federal cavalry was supposed to be in Virginia or well on its way there – according to Morgan's scouts. Instead they were active in Kentucky.

The fight at Mount Sterling was long and telling with the Confederates losing heavily; but the Northern cavalry was so crippled that pursuit of the routed Confederates was impossible. Morgan brought the main body from Lexington to support his defeated detachment.

On June 10th Morgan left Mount Sterling and entered Lexington again where some Federal depots were burned. From Lexington he galloped to Georgetown and then toward Cynthiana.

At dawn on June 11, 1864 General Morgan approached Cynthiana with his cavalry. The town itself was defended by a detachment of the 168th Ohio Infantry and some home guards – about 300 men – under the command of Colonel Conrad Garis. Morgan divided his troops into three columns, surrounded the town, and launched an attack at the covered bridge, driving Garis' forces back towards the railroad depot and then north along the railroad. The Confederates set fire to the town and destroyed many buildings.

When the Union garrison had surrendered, Morgan was informed that another force had moved into the outskirts of the town. He rode toward their reported position and discovered a Federal detachment of 750 men of the 171st Ohio under the command of Brigadier General Edward Hobson arrived by train about a mile north of the Cynthiana at Keller's Bridge. This regiment fought Morgan's force for about six hours. Eventually Morgan trapped this new Union force in a meander of the Licking River. Altogether, Morgan had about 1,300 Union prisoners of war camping with him overnight in line of battle. The 171st Ohio Infantry was paroled the next day. This engagement, Morgan's last victory, was known as the Battle of Keller's Bridge.

It is of some interest that Morgan and Hobson met again in this engagement. It was Hobson who had been the Union general who had run down Morgan in his Great Raid.

As night approached General Morgan committed one of his few tactical errors – some say the first in his brilliant career. (*Headley, p198*) Morgan encamped his 1,500 men along a road just thirty miles from Mount Sterling where Major General Stephen Burbridge from Georgetown, Kentucky, had 2,400 Federals – the 168th

Ohio and the rest of the 171st Ohio Regiments, some Michigan cavalry, and the Harrison County element of the Kentucky Home Guard.

The Union forces attacked at daybreak on June 12th. With little ammunition, Morgan recklessly decided to stay and fight. The Union forces drove the Rebels back, causing them to flee into town, where many were captured or killed. General Morgan and many of his officers escaped to Abingdon Virginia. (*Speed, p239*) Union casualties were 1,092 men; Morgan is estimated to have lost about 1,000 men. Thus ended General Morgan's fourth raid.

In Virginia, Morgan and his command were charged with robbing the Bank of Mount Sterling and undertaking the raid without proper authority. The recollection of Confederate Senator – later U.S. Senator – Benjamin H. Hill to Lieutenant J.W. Headley refutes the notion that Morgan acted without orders:

> *I remember very distinctly many of the facts for the manner as well as a matter stated by Mr. Davis (President) was very impressive. "Long ago," said the President, "I ordered Morgan to make this movement upon Sherman's rear and suggested that his best plan was to go directly from Abingdon through East Tennessee. But Morgan insisted that, if he were permitted to go through Kentucky and around Nashville, he could greatly recruit his horses and his men by volunteers. I yielded and allowed him to have his own way.* (Headley, p208)

As to the bank robbery charges, little was ever made of them. In the last letter that Morgan wrote, he spoke of the charges and said to the Confederate Secretary of War, Mr. Seddon, "I will demand a prompt and thorough investigation of [all the charges.]" (*Duke, p535*)

Morgan's adjutant, J.L. Sanford says, "The determination to pursue and break the general down was apparent to everyone and the Kentucky expedition was to be the means to accomplish this end." (*Letter to Basil Duke quoted in the* History of Morgan's Cavalry)

On September 3, 1864, General Morgan was at the home of a Mrs. Williams of Greenville, Tennessee. This lady had one son – a lieutenant – in the Union army and one in the Confederate. A short time before Morgan had discovered there a Union officer, who was recovering from wounds and paroled by the Confederates, attempting to get a note with information concerning Morgan's location through to Union officers. The note was discovered in the prayer book belonging to the wife of the young lieutenant. Morgan sent him under arrest to Abingdon. (*Holland, p340*)

On the previous night, Morgan had given orders to begin a march toward Bull's Gap at daybreak. Just before dawn Morgan countermanded the orders and a new time was set – seven o'clock in the morning. Between dawn and 7:00 AM a Federal detachment swept into town and charged the Williams' house. General Morgan, Major Gassett, and Captain Withers tried to reach their horses in the stable, but were cut off.

They then took shelter under a church on the opposite side of the block from the stables. Withers was sent back to the house to see if there were any avenue of escape, and he saw that there was none.

Meanwhile, the Union troops were breaking in the door of the church above Morgan. He and the two aides dashed for the house and as he ran through the shrubbery a woman shouted, "That's him! That's Morgan over there among the grape vines!" *(Holland, p345)*

Morgan shouted, "Don't shoot! I surrender!" He was immediately shot down.

Colonel Duke says only, "General Morgan was killed in the garden – shot through the heart. It is not known whether he surrendered or was offering resistance." *(Duke, p539)* The body of Morgan was thrown over a mule and paraded through town until it was recovered and sent to the Confederate lines by General Gillem, who commanded the Federal troops in the area.

When Morgan went down, there was great rejoicing in the North and great sadness in the South. Vitriolic statements appeared in the Northern newspapers and congratulations were sent to the troops who disposed of him. The south had lost a great leader and a symbol. As Duke puts it, "When he died, the glory and chivalry seemed gone from the struggle, and it became a tedious routine, enjoined by duty, and sustained by sentiments of pride and hatred." *(Duke, p 540)*

"He became one of the romantic figures of the war; and in death as in life he was a symbol of a way of life which ended on a Sabbath morning at Appomattox." *(Holland, p 353)*

None other than General U.S. Grant observes:

> *During 1863 and [186]4, John H. Morgan, a partisan officer, of no military education, but possessed of courage and endurance, operated in the rear of the Army of the Ohio in Kentucky and Tennessee. During the time he was operating in this way he killed, wounded, and captured several times the number he ever had under his command at any one time. He destroyed many millions of property in addition. Places he did not attack had to be guarded as if threatened by him.* (U.S. Grant, *Personal Memoirs*, volume II, p504)

The death of Morgan was a real blow to the spirit of the Confederacy, but the war moved relentlessly on. Basil Duke was made a Brigadier General and took command of the remnant of Morgan's Division on September 15, 1864.

Under the command of Duke the troops, now hardly more than a brigade, fought on many occasions. At Lick Creek, Carter's Station, and Saltville the men did justice to their reputation as soldiers and held the enemy at bay.

Now the fateful year of 1865 had dawned for the Confederacy. The end was not far off. Richmond fell. General A.P. Hill was killed. Lee surrendered. Discipline dissolved.

Orders came for all cavalry commanders to march for North Carolina. General Duke describes the scene:

> *I obtained permission to mount my men on mules. My command was about six hundred strong. The rain was falling in torrents when we prepared to start upon a march which seemed fraught with*

*danger. The men were drenched and mounted upon mules without saddles, and with blind bridles or rope halters. Everything conspired to remind them of the gloomy situation. We moved off in silence.* (Duke, p570)

At Charlotte, North Carolina, Jefferson Davis and his cabinet met the cavalry and set out for Alabama to meet Forrest and Taylor. At Abbeville, in South Carolina, a council of war was called. Present were President Davis, Generals Bragg and Breckenridge, and the brigade commanders Ferguson, Debrell, Vaughn, and Duke.

The consensus of opinion was that the troops would help Davis escape, but would not continue the struggle against unbeatable odds. Davis was heart-broken and tried to prevail upon the generals to hold on until the panic had passed. He felt that 2,500 men were enough to hold for the present. The council was silent and the President of the Confederacy arose and left the room.

The war was over The troops of John Hunt Morgan of Kentucky had stayed to the end. "There was no humiliation for these men. They had done their part and served faithfully, until there was no longer a cause or a country to serve." *(Duke, p 578)*

# WILLIAM WOODROW SLIDER

## ORIGINAL BIBLIOGRAPHY

Boling W.W., "Morgan's Visit to Brandenburg," *The Meade County Messenger*, April 11, 1946.

Duke, Basil W., *History of Morgan's Cavalry*, 1867.

Grant, U.S., *Personal Memoirs*, Volume II, 1886.

Headley, John W., *Confederate Operations in Canada and New York*, 1886.

Henry, Robert Selph, *The Story of the Confederacy*, 1943

Holland, Cecil Fletcher, *Morgan and His Raiders*, 1942

Gray, Wood, *The Hidden Civil War*, 1942.

Johnson, J. Stoddard, *Confederate Military History*, Volume IX, 1899.

Jones, J.B., *A Rebel War Clerk's Diary*, Volumes, I and II, 1935.

Lee, R.E., *Recollections and Letters of Robert E. Lee*, 1904.

*Official Records of the Union and Confederate Navies in the War of the Rebellion*, Volumes I and II, Series II; Volumes I and II, Series IV, 1899.

*Official Records of the Union and Confederate Armies in the War of the Rebellion*, Volumes I and II, Series II; Volumes I and II, Series III, 1899.

Speed, Thomas, *The Union Cause in Kentucky*, 1907.

Stevens, Alexander H., *The War Between the States*, 1870.

Young, Bennett, H., *Confederate Wizards in the Saddle*, 1914.

## ABOUT THE AUTHOR AND EDITORS

Dr. William W. Slider, A.A., B.A., M.A., M.S. S.T.M, D.D., Th.D., was a United Methodist pastor in Louisville, Kentucky. Dr. Slider, who passed away in 2001, was married to Jean Elizabeth Wells Slider, who followed him to heaven in 2008. The editors of this work were Bill and Jean's two sons, John and Bob.

Dr. John Wesley Slider, B.A., M.Div., D.Min., retired as a United Methodist pastor in 2010, and became a Free Methodist pastor. John is also a retired Marine Lt. Colonel. He is married to Lillian Natalia Stewart Slider, and they have two adult children and one grandchild.

Robert MacGregor Slider, B.A., M.B.A, C.F.P., is an Executive Vice President with Central Bank of Kentucky. Bob is married to Laura Jean Larkin Slider. They have two adult children.

Robert, William, and John Slider

Printed in the USA
CPSIA information can be obtained
at www.ICGtesting.com
LVHW022346240524
781087LV00007B/428